Off Peak

Tranquil Rambles
in
North East Derbyshire

by Michael Hull

SCARTHIN BOOKS
Cromford, Derbyshire
1998

Acknowledgements

Thanks are due to Heather, my wife, who accompanied me on several of these walks and helped "test drive" several of my route descriptions. I should also apologise for my many absences in front of the computer screen and at Chesterfield Library. Thanks to Martin for his help with printing some of the photographs. I would also like to thank Roy and Lynne for the impromptu brainstorming session that resulted in a much better title for the book. The staff at Chesterfield Local Studies Library were most helpful, but this book would have been finished much sooner if the library stayed open on Saturday afternoons!

Mike Hull, November 1997.

ISBN 0 97758 99 1
Published by Scarthin Books, Cromford, Derbyshire, 1988
Printed by Redwood Books
Text, Maps and Illustrations
© 1998 by Michael Hull
Designed and typeset by Masson Multimedia, Bonsall, Derbyshire

Contents

Introduction

I started this book in 1995 as a way of helping myself to regain fitness following an operation. It was something I had long wanted to do, as I derive so much pleasure from walking. Previously, I had never felt I had the time to write a book of walks, but luckily I found myself with two months off work to recuperate and the summer of 1995 also happened to be one of the best for many years. This provided me with the motivation to get started. I began with the shortest and easiest walks and gradually built up my fitness. I completed twelve of the walks within that time. Although the remaining walks took somewhat longer to complete, they were no less enjoyable.

Actually writing, rewriting, editing, researching historical facts and revising the book has taken far longer than I would have envisaged at the outset. Whilst writing and researching this book, I have spent many pleasurable hours retracing previous favourite walks and discovering many new places besides. In the process, I have learnt a great deal about my local area and I hope that you gain something of this from reading the book and following the walks.

I chose to concentrate on North East Derbyshire not only because it is close to home, but also because the area is usually overlooked in favour of the nearby Peak District National Park. Whilst the local scenery is more gentle and may not be as spectacular some parts of the Peak Park, North East Derbyshire has many treats in store. What is more, with only a few exceptions, you will find the walks are much less frequented and more peaceful than those in the Peak Park.

You will also be impressed with the quiet beauty of the district.

The walks are all very accessible from Sheffield, Chesterfield, Matlock and surrounding towns. The walks north of Chesterfield are around the Holmesfield, Barlow and Eckington areas. The walks to the west and south of Chesterfield are principally around Linacre, Holymoorside and Ashover. Some of the walks are just within the Peak District National Park, and some stray into South Yorkshire briefly, but by and large all are within the boundaries of North East Derbyshire district.

For most of the walks you do not need to be particularly fit and you can take things at a leisurely pace if you wish. Only a few of the walks are more strenuous and I have given a summary of the type of terrain that is encountered, including any long or steep climbs, at the start of each chapter.

The timings given do not allow for rests and lunch stops, etc so you need to allow extra time if you intend to have a picnic or stop off at a pub on the way. The timings assume an average pace of about 2 miles (3 km) per hour. I have given information about pubs and refreshment stops en route (or within a short distance of the route). Not all of these will be open at lunchtime (especially mid week and in the winter), so if you intend to rely upon them to provide you with liquid and edible sustenance, it would be as well to check in advance to avoid disappointment.

I recommend good quality walking boots or shoes that offer sufficient ankle support. In the dry summer months you may get by with training shoes, but at all other times most of these walks can be very muddy and slippery. Also, remember that the British climate is fickle and unpredictable, so take waterproof clothing and a spare layer in case it turns wet or cold.

The sketch maps are provided only to help identify the route and are not intended to replace an Ordnance Survey map. The recommended maps for each of the walks are listed elsewhere, but the most useful are the following:

Pathfinder 761 - Chesterfield (SK 36/37) 1:25,000 scale

Outdoor Leisure 24 - The Peak District - White Peak Area 1:25,000 scale.

By and large the paths are in a reasonable state, although some paths will be muddy or overgrown at certain times of the year. Some landowners take it upon themselves to make life difficult for walkers. If you find your way blocked, or find that a stile has been removed, please write to the Public Rights of Way Officer at North East Derbyshire District Council, Saltergate, Chesterfield, noting the date that you encountered the obstruction and providing the relevant map reference. It would be a good idea to take a photograph if you have a camera handy. Even if you find your way blocked, please keep to the Country Code, which is set out below.

Please note that, although I have tried to ensure the utmost accuracy in describing these walks and drawing the sketch maps, it is inevitable that certain features will change with the passage of time, especially man-made things, such as stiles and fences etc.

It was a pleasure to write this book and I hope that you will gain as much enjoyment from these walks as I did.

The Country Code

1. Enjoy the countryside and respect its life and work
2. Guard against all risk of fire
3. Fasten all gates
4. Keep your dogs under close control
5. Keep to public paths across farmland
6. Use gates and stiles to cross fences, hedges and walls
7. Leave livestock, crops and machinery alone
8. Take your litter home
9. Help to keep all water clean
10. Protect wildlife, plants and trees
11. Take special care on country roads
12. Make no unnecessary noise

Metric Conversion

1 kilometre = 0.6214 mile
1 yard = 0.9144 metre

1 mile = 1.6093 kilometres
1 metre = 1.0936 yards

Map References and how to use them.

Example - Cartledge Hall, Holmesfield (SK323773)

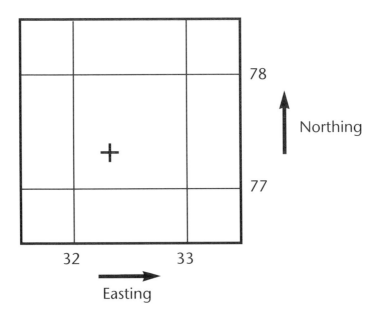

The SK prefix refers to a 100 km grid square and needn't concern us here, as all the walks are within the SK grid square. There are two other main components to a map reference, eastings and northings. The easting is the first 3 numbers and the northing is the last 3.

The easting is taken by reading the grid numbers along the bottom edge of the map, in this case the relevant number is 32, which gives the first two numbers of the easting. The third number is found by estimating tenths of the square, and this case we estimate 3 tenths as the full easting is 323. Follow a similar procedure for northings up the right hand side of the map. In this case we are looking for gridline 77 and then again 3 tenths up, as the full northing is 773.

By combining the easting and the northing you can locate a point within an area 100m x 100m.

I have included a map reference in the introduction of each walk to help you locate the exact starting point.

Recommended Maps

Walks 1, 2, 4, 5, 6, 7, 12, 13, 14, and 19: Outdoor Leisure 24 (White Peak)

Walks 1, 2, 3, 4, 5, 11, 12, 13, 14, 15, 16, 17, 19 and 20: Pathfinder 761 (Chesterfield)

Walk 8 ideally requires: Pathfinder 761, 743, 744 and 762

Walk 9: Pathfinder 744 and 762

Walk 10: Pathfinder 761 and 762

Walk 18: Pathfinder 761 and 794 (Crich)

All the above are at 1:25,000 scale (4 cm to a kilometre or 2.5 inches to one mile), which is the best scale for walking. Alternatively, the Landranger 119 Buxton, Matlock & Dovedale map (1:50,000 scale) covers all the walks in this book, except Walk 8, which also requires Landrangers 110 and 120, Walk 10, which additionally requires Landranger 120 and Walk 9, which requires Landranger 120 only. However, these maps are to a smaller scale, have less detail and are harder to follow.

Public Transport

With the exception of Walks 6, 7, 11, 12, 19 and 20, the start of each walk is accessible in some way by bus, although Walks 7, 11, 12 and 19 have buses which pass by within 500 yds. Obviously, the accessibility by bus is dependent upon where you are travelling from. I recommend the purchase of the North East Derbyshire Bus and Trains Timetable, published by Derbyshire County Council Public Transport Unit, Chatsworth Hall, Chesterfield Road, Matlock DE4 3FW. If you wish to confirm the times of any bus, you can telephone BUSLINE on Chesterfield (01246) 250450, between 0700 and 2000 daily. South Yorkshire Passenger Transport Executive (whose address is Exchange Street, Sheffield S2 5SZ) have a similar service called Traveline on Sheffield (0114) 276 8688. SYPTE also publish a timetable covering South Yorkshire.

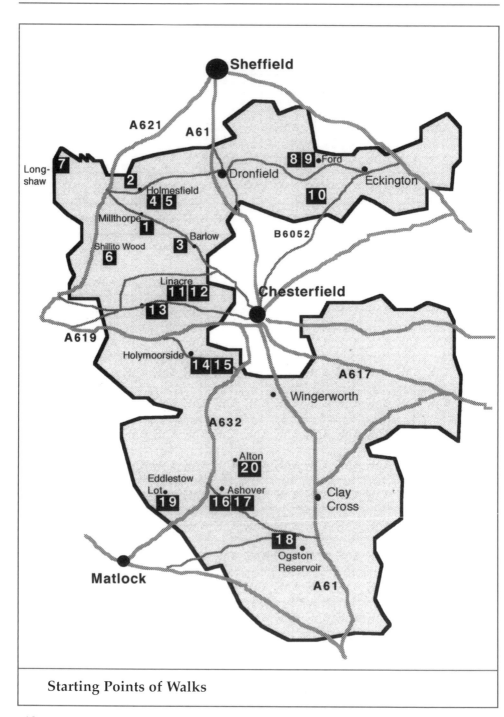

Starting Points of Walks

Key to symbols used on sketch maps

The route	
Optional route	
Other footpaths	
Roads	
Unmade roads/tracks	
Deciduous Woodland	
Evergreen Woodland	
Streams/rivers	
Reservoirs	
Churches	
Major buildings	
Quarries/ Workings	
Embankments	
Crags/Rockfaces	

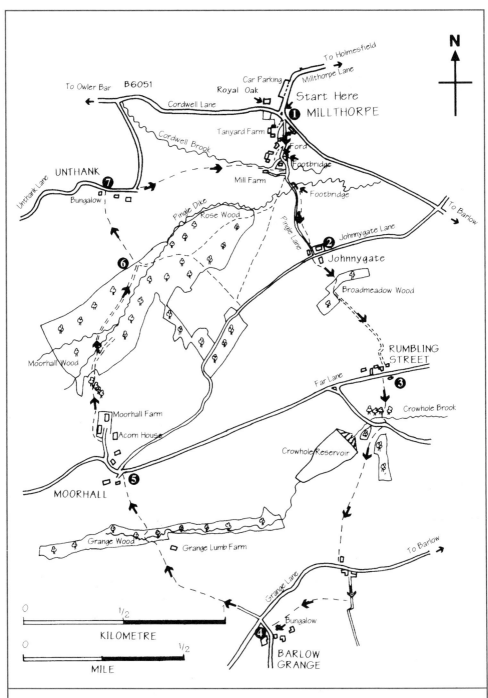

Walk 1 Millthorpe - Rumbling Street - Barlow Grange - Rose Wood - Unthank - Millthorpe

Route: Millthorpe - Rumbling Street - Barlow Grange - Rose Wood - Unthank - Millthorpe

Approximate distance: 4.5 miles (7 km)

Starting point: Millthorpe, outside Royal Oak pub

Map reference: SK317764

Required maps: OS Outdoor Leisure 24 (The White Peak) or Pathfinder 761 (Chesterfield) - both 1:25,000 scale. Alternatively, Landranger 119 (Buxton, Matlock and Dovedale) - 1:50,000 scale.

Terrain: Farmland, woodland, good views, some steep climbs, some paths muddy when wet.

Refreshments: Royal Oak pub, Millthorpe.

Approximate time: 2 hours 30 minutes

Public transport: Buses from Chesterfield and Holmesfield

The Walk

The walk starts near the Royal Oak pub in Millthorpe ❶. There is a small parking area at the bottom of Millthorpe Lane, close to the junction with Cordwell Lane (B6051).

From the Royal Oak take the narrow lane (Mill Lane) opposite the bottom of Millthorpe Lane, marked with a "No Through Road" sign. Follow the lane across the ford and continue on the other side past the entrance to Mill Farm, where it narrows. Proceed straight ahead between hedges and then downhill. At the bottom and if dry, continue along the sunken Pingle Lane uphill to Johnnygate ❷. (If it is wet, the lane will be a running stream so take the alternative path which breaks off near the small timber footbridge and runs parallel in the adjacent field on your left.)

Turn right onto Johnnygate Lane for 20 yds and then over the stile opposite (sign posted for Oxton Rakes). Follow the left hand edge of this field towards Broadmeadow Wood ahead. Follow the path through the wood for about 100 yds and onto a track which passes

Well Dressing, Millthorpe

through open farmland towards the farm at Rumbling Street ❸, on the crest of the hill directly ahead. Pass through the farmyard and take the footpath on the opposite side of Far Lane.

Follow the left hand side of the fields as you descend towards a stream and some trees. Near the bottom, go between a large tree and some bushes down to a footbridge across Crowhole Brook. The path then climbs uphill for 50 yds to a stile, which is just to the left of a large holly bush.

Turn right onto the lane for 30 yds and go through the gate on the left. Follow the path uphill, initially passing close to a small wood, which is on the right, and then into a steeply sloping field. At the top of the field there is an excellent view of Holmesfield, Blackamoor and Norton. Climb over the broken down dry stone wall (there was a stile here once) and cross the next field diagonally to the right. Pass between stone posts and follow the left hand edge of the next field towards stone farm buildings and onto the lane.

Turn left onto the lane for 25 yds and then right, through a small surfaced farmyard to a metal gate and then descend down the green lane ahead until it flattens out. Cross the stile on the right just after a solitary tree. Follow the right hand edge of the field for 150 yds and, as the field widens out, continue in a straight line across the centre of the field towards the stile, which is just to the left of a row of small trees and close to a timber electricity pole. If you look back, there are fine views of Chesterfield, Brampton, Walton and beyond.

Follow the path uphill across two fields towards a bungalow, which is adjacent to Barlow Grange ❹. At the lane, turn right towards the road junction. On the opposite side of the junction there is a stile and a gate leading to a track.

Follow the track straight ahead for about 250 yds, before crossing a stile next to a gate. Follow the right hand edge of the next field to a stone stile. The path now goes downhill diagonally to the right, passing through an archway in the holly bushes and then across two more fields towards Grange Wood, passing between stone flag posts into the wood. The path drops down to a footbridge across a deep stream and then climbs steeply up the opposite side, before emerging into fields once again.

Continue straight ahead over the crest and make towards the stone house ahead, crossing three fields. The path eventually passes just to the right of the house and its outbuildings, through a small white gate and to the lane at Moorhall ❺. Join the lane, turn left and follow it as it curves to the right and slightly uphill. After about 75 yds, leave the lane at the sharp left turn, following the sign posted footpath along the farm track, which is directly in front of you.

Follow the track past Moorgreen Farm and Acorn House for 100 yds before crossing the low stone stile on the left just before Moorhall Farm. Walk around the rear of the farm buildings towards the stone stile near the metal gate. Then head downhill, aiming just to the left of the line of small trees. Walk parallel to them, following the waymark posts, and then pass through a gap in the trees. Continue through a timber gate into Moorhall Wood.

Once in the wood, follow the track for 70 yds, before turning left and steeply downhill across the stream (be careful in wet weather as it can be slippery). Continue along the track for just over a quarter of a mile, until the path reaches the edge of the wood, where there is a stile to the left into open fields ❻.

Head straight across the field towards a gap leading into the next field. Keep to right and climb over the stile next to a

Grange Wood

View towards Holmesfield from near Unthank

five bar gate. Keep to left of the next field to reach Unthank Lane ❼. Turn right and follow the lane for 200 yds until it turns sharp left. At this point take the footpath straight ahead of you. Cross two fields keeping to the right hand side, eventually crossing a stile and continuing past a stone cottage and then between a stone wall and a garden fence. Emerge onto Mill Lane, turning left, cross the ford and retrace the first part of this walk into Millthorpe.

Places of Interest

Tanyard Farm - At one time, there were two tanneries in Millthorpe, hence the name of the farm. One tannery was situated on the site of the present car park opposite the Royal Oak pub, the other was to the west along the Cordwell Valley.

The Mill - There used to be a corn mill in Millthorpe, which harnessed water power to grind corn. It was located quite close to the ford across Millthorpe Brook. The mill was still in operation just before World War II, but only for the production of animal feed. In part, the mill declined due to poor maintenance of the mill dam, which meant that there was not always enough force available to power the wheel. Also, with the introduction of modern farming machinery, farmers were able to grind their own corn. The mill was eventually demolished in 1971 and houses were built on the site.

Pingle Lane (also known as Mill Lane) - This is an ancient "hollow way", ie a lane worn hollow with centuries of use. At some points, Pingle Lane is a good 10 feet below the level of the surrounding fields.

Rumbling Street - This is a small settlement on Far Lane, which is comprised of a farm, various barns and a couple of houses. One of the barns contains two ancient crucks. It stands end on to the lane. The present farmhouse, which has its origins in the Tudor period, superseded the cruck building as a residence. Far Lane has its origins in Roman times, when it was built to transport pigs of lead ore to Chesterfield. Possibly the name 'Rumbling Street' has some connection to the noise made by the passing traffic.

Barlow Grange - Barlow Grange is a fine 17th century farmhouse, which is Grade II listed.

Rose Wood - In May 1970, a US Phantom fighter bomber crashed into these woods, leaving a crater 20 ft deep. The impact was near ❻ on the map and was apparently very dramatic. The two airmen on board had ejected over Froggatt and Calver, but the plane flew for another five miles before hitting the ground.

Unthank - The name 'Unthank' is believed to be derived from the Anglo-Saxon word 'Unpanc' which means "ill will", indicating that at some point in the past there were squatters occupying this area. Another (unlikely) theory put forward is that the name is derived from 'Hun's Thwong' - Hun being a personal name and a thwong being an area of land measured out with a thong of leather.

The Royal Oak, Millthorpe

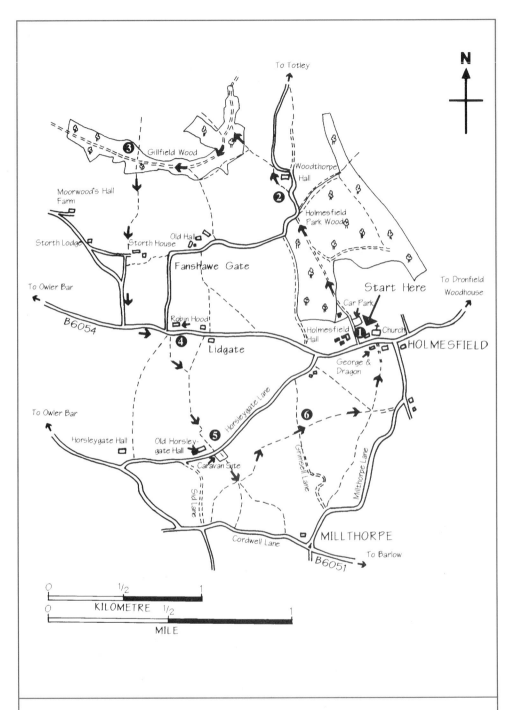

Walk 2 Holmesfield - Woodthorpe Hall - Robin Hood - Horsleygate Lane - Holmesfield

Route: Holmesfield - Woodthorpe Hall - Robin Hood - Horsleygate Lane - Holmesfield

Approximate distance: 3.75 miles (6 km)

Starting point: Holmesfield church (St. Swithins)

Map reference: SK317764

Required maps: OS Outdoor Leisure 24 (The White Peak) or Pathfinder 761 (Chesterfield) - both 1:25,000 scale. Alternatively, Landranger 119 (Buxton, Matlock and Dovedale) - 1:50,000 scale.

Terrain: Woodland, farmland, meadowland, good views. Two lengthy climbs.

Refreshments: The Angel, The George and Dragon, Holmesfield; The Robin Hood, Lidgate

Approximate time: 2 hours.

Public transport: Buses from Sheffield, Dronfield and Chesterfield.

The Walk

This walk starts at St. Swithins church, Holmesfield ❶. Parking is possible on Park Avenue in the church car park. There are two public houses here - The Angel and The George & Dragon.

From the main road, turn down Park Avenue, between The Angel and Holmesfield Hall. Continue to the end of the road (200 yds) and take the path directly ahead, with open fields to the right and a hedge to the left. Enter Holmesfield Park Wood and follow the broad track downhill for a third of a mile until Fanshaw Gate Lane is reached. Follow the lane to the right and around a left bend. After about 150 yds, take the sign posted path on the left, keeping to the right of the field to a stile. Remain to the

St. Swithins Church

right as you pass below the grounds of Woodthorpe Hall ❷ to the next stile. Bear slightly left between bushes for 25 yds, over a stile and head downhill, towards the trees at the bottom and then into the wood.

Cross a footbridge and shortly afterwards turn left, joining a broad path. The path twists and turns at first, but then straightens out somewhat. Continue for nearly half a mile and look carefully for a "crossroads" where another path crosses at 90° ❸.

Turn left, downhill and over another footbridge into a field. Proceed uphill and at the top left hand corner of the field, pass through the gap and bear half left towards a timber post only 25 yds away. Once past this post, continue uphill towards the sinister-looking Storth House. At the top of the field, cross the stile just to the right of the house. Turn right onto the farmyard track and after 25 yds take the left turning up another track. After about 200 yds join Moorwood Lane (metalled road) and upon reaching the main road, cross over and turn left uphill towards the Robin Hood pub ❹.

Just below the crest of the hill and opposite the Robin Hood, take the second sign posted path on the right ("Horsleygate Hall 1/2"). Keep to the left of the field. Cross the stone stile and head half left across the field. The path is not wholly distinct, so keep the village of Barlow in the distance in your sights.

After about 250 yds the path joins another from Lidgate. Turn half right on this path, go through a large metal gate and continue downhill. At the end of the field, the path turns 90° to the right for 40 yds and then back downhill. Cross another field, passing behind a house (Old Horsleygate Hall) with a tennis court, and emerge onto Horsleygate Lane ❺. (At this point, it is worth just walking down the lane for a few yards to admire the frontage of the Hall and then retrace your steps.)

Turn left for 40 yds and then cross the stile on the right. Pass downhill straight through the caravan site to the stile at the bottom. Continue downhill for about 75 yds to the bottom left corner of the field. Cross the stile and footbridge into the field on the left. Climb diagonally to the stile about halfway along on the top boundary.

Continue uphill for a short distance, then bear slightly to the right and cross to the stone stile. Keep parallel with the bottom of the next field, then cross the following field to the wooden stile. Wade across the sunken lane (known as Grimsell Lane) ❻ and go through the wooden gate. Continue ahead, crossing three fields, in the third field heading towards the stile

View of Cordwell Valley from near Holmesfield

below the leftmost tree ahead of you. Cross the centre of the following field, and turn left at the far end, proceeding uphill to a stile next to a gate. Then, keep to the left as you ascend, reaching a stile which leads onto a grassy lane. Continue past the George and Dragon pub to the main road and the end of your walk.

Places of Interest

St Swithins Church - A church has stood on this spot since Anglo-Saxon times, but the present church was erected in 1826. The chancel was added in 1895.

The Angel - The original Angel was the brewhouse of the lord of the manor and was a low building with stone and metal vats for brewing. This was replaced in the mid 19th century by the building that preceded the present pub. Holmesfield parish has so many pubs because of the turnpiking of the road through the village in 1845. The village became a convenient stopping off point on the Gleadless - Calver - Stoney Middleton Turnpike.

Holmesfield Hall

The George & Dragon - This building was originally a farmhouse although it was simultaneously an alehouse. Part of the original construction still survives.

Holmesfield Hall (Holmesfield Hall Farm) - The building on the right as you look from the road is possibly on the site of the original Anglian aula (hall) and has recently been converted into houses. The present day Hall stands at the rear left hand corner of the site. In the 17th century, the present façade was added, which incorporates the coat of arms of the Burtons, a prosperous family, several members of which were sheriffs of Derbyshire during that period.

Holmesfield Park Wood - This is ancient woodland, which in previous centuries was a deer park for the manor of Holmesfield. Today, it forms part of the estate of Woodthorpe Hall.

Woodthorpe Hall - A fine 17th century manor house, built by the Fanshawes, who moved here from Fanshawe Gate Hall. The Fanshawes were very prominent in local life for several centuries, although the family eventually moved away to other landholdings in south Derbyshire. Dronfield School (now known as Henry Fanshawe School) was founded by Henry Fanshawe, who was Queen's Remembrancer of the Exchequer in the reign of Elizabeth I. He was the first of nine Fanshawes to hold this position. In a ceremony which takes place to this day, the Remembrancer receives from the City of London Solicitor a 'quit-rent' of six horseshoes, 61 nails, a hatchet and a billhook for land rented from the Crown by the City of London. Much of the stonework and timber in Woodthorpe Farm, which adjoins Woodthorpe Hall, came from the largely dismantled Fanshawe Gate Hall. Woodthorpe Hall has been added to very little since it was built. In recent times it has been restored by the Shepley family and is a focus for village events such as outdoor operatic extravaganzas and fireworks displays.

Storth House - A farm has stood on this site since at least the 13th century. The farmhouse is several centuries old, although it has been modernised. The farm buildings are even older - probably dating from Tudor times.

The Robin Hood - Standing on a windswept hilltop, this pub was originally just a small alehouse. However, with the turnpiking of the road and the construction of a nearby tollhouse (now demolished), trade increased and the pub was extended. Today, the pub is a destination in itself for those seeking food and refreshment.

Old Horsleygate Hall - This is the original Horsleygate Hall, the newer 'Hall' being an enlarged farmhouse located further down the lane. Until comparatively recently, the Hall was in a very sorry state of repair, but it has now been renovated. In 1806, the Hall was damaged by a terrible fire, which destroyed several outbuildings, killed cattle and burned corn and hay. Apparently, some timbers within the building still display signs of fire damage. Parts of the building date from the 15th century or earlier. The derelict stone barn on the south side of the lane, with triangular 'windholes', is of great age.

Old Horsleygate Hall

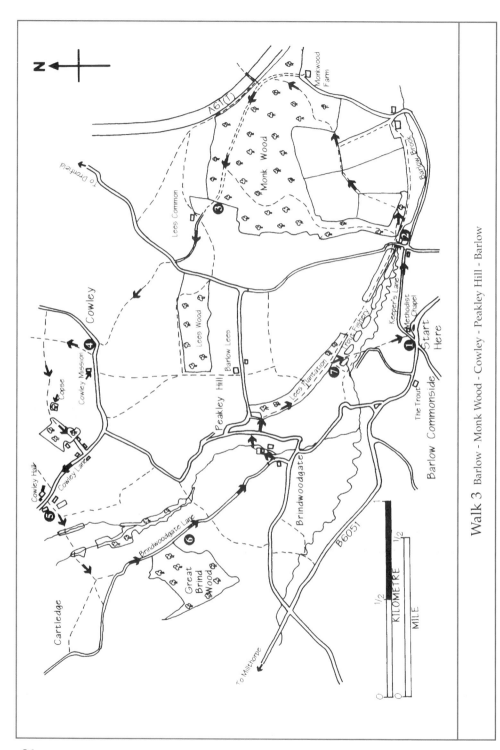

Walk 3 Barlow - Monk Wood - Cowley - Peakley Hill - Barlow

Route: Barlow - Monk Wood - Cowley - Peakley Hill - Barlow

Approximate distance: 5.25 miles (8 km)

Starting point: Barlow (Commonside) adjacent to Methodist Chapel on Millcross Lane.

Map reference: SK 340754.

Required maps: OS Pathfinder 761 (Chesterfield) - 1:25,000 scale. Alternatively, Landranger 119 (Buxton, Matlock and Dovedale) - 1:50,000 scale.

Terrain: Woodland, farmland, mainly good paths and tracks. Easy going, some very short climbs.

Refreshments: The Trout, Barlow Commonside

Approximate time: 2 hours 30 minutes

Public transport: Buses from Chesterfield.

The Walk

The walk starts from Barlow, which has two centres. This walk starts from the northerly part, Commonside, about 200 yds east of The Trout public house. Near the Methodist chapel on Millcross Lane, there is a loop in the road, which makes an ideal lay-by to park in ❶.

From this point head towards the centre of Commonside for only a few yards and turn acute right down Keeper's Lane. Continue for just over quarter of a mile to the end and turn left, crossing the hump backed bridge ❷. Turn sharp right and after 50 yds half left over a small wooden footbridge. Look out for yellow arrows on the trees and follow these diagonally to the right up a bank through the trees.

Emerge into a field and strike out half right, aiming for the top right hand corner, which may not be visible at first during summer months. Once at the top, go through the gate on the right and follow the left side of the next field. At the far end, cross the stile on the left and follow the right hand side of the next field towards the wood. Cross the wooden stile into the wood and follow the narrow, but distinct, path as it zig zags through the wood. After about quarter of a mile, the path emerges onto a woodland track. Turn left and follow this track all the way through Monk Wood. After about another quarter of a mile or so, reach a five bar gate. Pass through and continue along the track, which at this point has a lovely view over to the west ❸. Go through the gate marked "Private Road - Footpath Only" and follow the road downhill until reaching the public road.

Cross the road and take the footpath directly opposite. Keep to the left of the first field and then head half right across the second, reaching a wide gap leading into the next field. Keep to the right through this and the following field, noticing a tennis court over on your left as you reach the end of the field. Cross the stile in the far right hand corner and turn left onto Cowley Lane for 50 yds before turning right over a stile near a blue gate (which may be hard to spot in the summer) ❹. Keep to the right of the field and at the end, where several paths cross, turn left. Then cross two fields keeping initially to the left, before heading just to the right of the

View across Cordwell Valley from Brindwoodgate Lane

nearest piece of woodland. The path passes to the right of the small wood and then curves left in front of the next wood. Stay on the path and pass a bungalow, a stone barn and a house before reaching Cowley Lane and turning right.

After 250 yds, opposite Cowley Hall ❺ and just after passing a timber open barn, turn left along a path sign posted "Holmesfield". The path passes a manege (dressage ring), then goes into a field. Keep to the right hand side and go down towards trees in the dip. Follow the path out of the other side, across the field, through another dip with a band of trees. Head diagonally left across the next field to a metal stile near a five bar gate. Turn half left downhill towards a gate 100 yds away. Turn right for 10 yds, go through a gate and onto a wide track. Turn left and follow this lane (Brindwoodgate Lane) downhill for two thirds of a mile, passing woodland ❻ and gaining occasional extensive views.

Upon reaching a gate, continue for 75 yds and then turn sharp left onto another track, which takes you past a house and a garden, with a large pond, and then close to an annex and garage. Behind the annex, take the steps up the bank into the trees. Cross the stile, turn right up more steps and continue up the grassy bank (very slippery when wet) to the stone stile. Turn right onto the lane for 50 yds and take the track on the left between the bench and the post box. Follow this for 75 yds and bear right through the gate.

Follow the path along the bottom fringe of woodland for just over quarter of a mile and then bear right downhill at a stile and head towards the fishing lakes ❼. Pass between the first and second lakes, then cross the footbridge and go up through a stile. After 50 yds, emerge onto a lane, and shortly afterwards turn left through a stile near a green gate. Keep to the right of two fields as you proceed uphill past modern houses. Emerge onto Keeper's Lane, turn right and follow it a short distance back to your starting point.

Places of Interest

Barlow Commonside - Commonside is at some remove from Barlow village itself, and was originally a 19th century addition, brought about by the mining industry. Since the Second World War, there have been further additions and Commonside now houses most of the population of Barlow.

Mining - It is difficult to credit from present day appearances, but until the early 1960s, Barlow was a mining village. At one time there were 14 pits and 15 open cast sites within the local area. Many of the operations were on a very small scale, but nonetheless mining dominated the village. Today, the village is a pleasant residential area with most people working in nearby Chesterfield or Sheffield.

Monk Wood - There was a colliery within Monk Wood in the late 19th century, with an incline to transport the coal down to the valley bottom. As long ago as the 12th century, the Monks of Louth monastery (hence the name "Monk Wood") gave permission for the locals to work ironstone in the wood and to have two furnaces, one for smelting iron, the other for hammering and forging. Today, the traces of the industrial past are still to be found, but the wood is now managed for its timber rather than for its mineral wealth.

Cowley Mission - Built in 1893, this tiny Methodist chapel is still use. There had been a Methodist congregation for many years and meetings had been held at Schoolwood Cottage nearby, before enough money was raised to build the present chapel.

Cowley Hall - The house has a long history and many former outbuildings have been demolished. The present façade is of 19th century origin.

Brindwoodgate - This lane, which is a bridleway today, was once a major route locally and also for packhorses. When Cartledge Grange was owned by the Abbey at Beauchief, Brindwoodgate was a comparatively busy road. It is believed that the woolpack transported from London to Eyam, which caused famous outbreak of the plague in Eyam, could possibly have passed along this way.

Trout Fishery - The trout fishery is on the site of the former Crowhole Colliery, which closed early in the 20th century.

Bridge across Barlow Brook

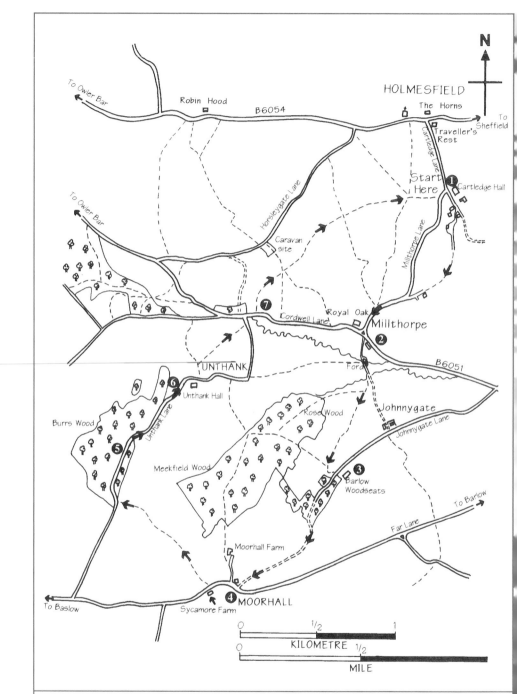

Walk 4 Cartledge Hall - Millthorpe - Barlow Woodseats - Moorhall - Burrs Wood - Unthank - Cartledge Hall

Route: Cartledge Hall - Millthorpe - Barlow Woodseats - Moorhall - Burrs Wood - Unthank - Cartledge Hall

Approximate distance: 5 miles (8 km)

Starting point: Cartledge Lane, Holmesfield outside Cartledge Hall. **Map reference:** SK323773.

Required maps: OS Outdoor Leisure 24 (The White Peak) or Pathfinder 761 (Chesterfield) - both 1:25,000 scale. Alternatively, Landranger 119 (Buxton, Matlock and Dovedale) - 1:50,000 scale.

Terrain: Oak and beech woodland as well as open farmland with fine views. Fairly easy going. Slightly hilly. Some lanes and paths very muddy in winter. This walk takes in several of the old halls of the area, none of which are open to the public.

Refreshments: The Royal Oak, Millthorpe.

Approximate time: 2 hours 30 minutes.

Public transport: Buses from Sheffield, Dronfield and Chesterfield.

The Walk

The walk starts on Cartledge Lane, Holmesfield outside Cartledge Hall ❶, a handsome mediaeval manor house. There are limited spaces on Cartledge Lane for parking on the field side of the road, but please bear in mind that Cartledge Lane is on a bus route, so park carefully.

Start by bearing left down the "No Through Road" past Cartledge Hall, and Cartledge Grange Farm. After 100 yds, bear right through the farmyard, passing Cartledge Cottage and Cartledge Hall Farm, and a bungalow with a large picture window on the right. Continue ahead, down the muddy lane to a stile. Cross the next field, keeping left, to a timber stile and through a private garden (don't worry, you are on a public

Cartledge Hall

footpath!) and follow the driveway to Millthorpe Lane, where you turn left down to Millthorpe ❷.

At Millthorpe, take the "No Through Road" opposite and follow the lane down past the ford and along the track until reaching a stone stile on the right in a wall marked "Mill Farm". Cross the stile, follow the left hand side of the first field and strike diagonally right in the second field towards the footbridge. Over the bridge, climb two stiles in quick succession and follow the left side of the field uphill to the stile. Keep to the right of the next field for about 100 yds and then strike half left towards a gap in the trees. Cross the stream (note, very muddy in winter) and head up the bank half left to the gate, emerging onto the lane opposite Barlow Woodseats ❸.

Turn right onto Johnnygate Lane and follow the winding lane through attractive oak and beech woodland. After two thirds of a mile emerge onto the road at Moorhall ❹.

Bear right, following the road round right and left bends. Just before reaching Sycamore Farm, take the footpath on the right over the somewhat hidden stone stile. Initially, bear slightly left and cross the stile which is to the left of a small tree. Then keep to the right, pass through the gate at the end. After another 75 yds cross the stile and head diagonally uphill to the stone stile at the far left of the wall on the near horizon. Keep left across the next two fields, cross a small field and head downhill towards woodland. Look out for the small wooden stile near the field entrance and emerge onto Unthank Lane.

Turn right and head downhill through pleasant woodland (Burrs Wood). After about quarter of a mile, there is a gate on the left with a "Woodland Trust" sign ❺. If you wish, you can explore this wood, but be prepared for thick undergrowth, steep and slippery slopes and indistinct paths and take care not to damage the plants and undergrowth. Otherwise, stay on the lane until turning onto a footpath on the left opposite the entrance to Unthank Hall ❻.

Follow the stone wall closely and where the wall turns full right, ignore the path that continues downhill, swing round half right and cross the stile left of the chestnut tree. Keep to the right and head for the gap at the end of the field, before heading diagonally left down the ramp to the stile near the white gate. Turn left onto the lane, and then right at the T-junction. After about 75 yds, look out for the signpost on the left (covered by bushes in summer) and go up the stone steps to the stile ❼.

Proceed uphill along the left of the field for 200 yds, then bear diagonally right to a gap in the hedge. Continue diagonally uphill to the top corner of the field, cross the stile beneath the trees and go over the footbridge. Cross the next field diagonally to the left, up to the stile halfway along the top boundary of the field.

Continue uphill for a short distance, then

Barlow Woodseats

bear slightly to the right and cross to the low stone stile. Stay parallel with the bottom of the next field, and continue across the following field to the wooden stile. Cross the sunken track and go through the wooden gate. Continue ahead, across three fields, in the third field heading towards the stile below the leftmost tree in front of you. Cross the centre of the following field, go through the gate ahead, across the footbridge and uphill. After a short distance, join a muddy lane, and then emerge onto the top end of Millthorpe Lane. Turn left and walk the few yards back to your starting point.

Places of Interest

Cartledge Hall - The present house is reputed to date from 1492, when it was built by a John Wolstenholme (who originally came from Rochdale), but there are some parts of the building which may predate this period. According to local historian, the late Bessie Bunker, there is evidence that an aula (hall) was established here in the 6th century by Anglian settlers. This would have been a building built entirely of timber and with just one chamber, where the lord would have dwelt with his retinue. The present house has massive oak timbers, oak panelled walls and has ornate plaster moulded ceilings which date from about 1610. (More about Cartledge Hall can be found in the next chapter.)

Cartledge Grange - Legend has it that Cartledge Grange was built in a fit of family pique, as it blocks the views that Cartledge Hall would have otherwise enjoyed across the Cordwell valley. For a time and until the dissolution of the monasteries by Henry VIII, the monks of Beauchief Abbey had a farm at Cartledge Grange. The property was extended in the early 18th century by the Jolly family.

Barlow Woodseats - The name "Woodseats" is derived from Old English, "wudu" and "saete", meaning "dwellings in the wood". In 1270, Jordan de Barley granted Adam Francis some land and he built a house. This predated the present building, which was largely built in the early 17th century by Arthur Mower, chief agent to the Barleys. The Barleys were the major landowners of the area around Barlow (and, indeed, took their name from the village), although they fell on hard times and left the area for good at about the time Arthur Mower was building the house. Today we see an impressive stone manor house and farm with mullioned and transomed windows. The large cruck barn was the original hall. It was hit by a stray Luftwaffe bomb in 1941, but has since been restored.

Moor Hall - Moor Hall Farm, was built by the Foljambes in the early Tudor period, although there is evidence of a settlement here from pre Norman times.

Burrs Wood - Burrs Wood, which stands on the steep sides of Unthank Bank has been acquired by the Woodland Trust, in whose care the trees and wildlife are protected. The public are free to wander through these woods, but beware! There are no proper paths and the thick undergrowth and steep slopes made the going very difficult.

Unthank Hall - Although very much a working farm, Unthank Hall is of great antiquity. As at Cartledge Hall, there are ornate plaster ceilings, which are thought to be the work of the same craftsman. There is a substantial barn, which has five surviving cruck timbers of great antiquity and this has recently been restored. Around Unthank Hall, there is evidence of ridge-and-furrow ploughing.

View towards Holmesfield from near Sycamore Farm

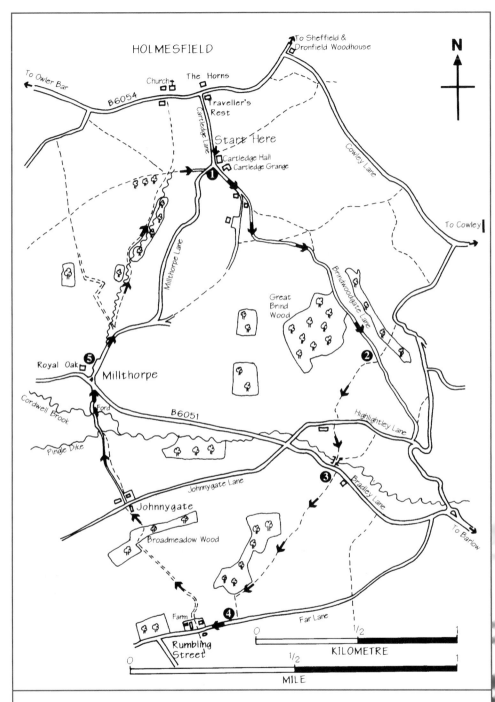

Walk 5 Cartledge Hall - Great Brind Wood - Far Lane - Johnnygate - Millthorpe - Cartledge Hall

Route: Cartledge Hall - Great Brind Wood - Far Lane - Johnnygate - Millthorpe - Cartledge Hall

Approximate distance: 4 miles (6.5 km)

Starting point: Cartledge Lane, Holmesfield outside Cartledge Hall.

Map reference: SK323773.

Required maps: OS Outdoor Leisure 24 (The White Peak) or Pathfinder 761 (Chesterfield) - both 1:25,000 scale. Alternatively, Landranger 119 (Buxton, Matlock and Dovedale) - 1:50,000 scale.

Terrain: Lanes, farmland, woodland. Muddy in places when wet, otherwise not too difficult.

Refreshments: The Royal Oak, Millthorpe.

Approximate time: 2 hours.

Public transport: Buses from Sheffield, Dronfield and Chesterfield.

The Walk

The walk starts on Cartledge Lane, Holmesfield ❶ outside Cartledge Hall, a handsome mediaeval manor house. There are limited spaces on Cartledge Lane for parking on the field side of the road, but please bear in mind that Cartledge Lane is on a bus route, so park carefully.

Start by bearing left down the lane past Cartledge Hall, and Cartledge Grange Farm. Continue as the lane becomes unmetalled and follow downhill, first with views of Barlow and Unstone and then with views across the Cordwell valley. The lane curves left, then right and after about a third of a mile narrows and continues with bushes and trees to either side.

Cartledge Grange in winter

Pass Great Brind Wood (on your right hand side) and carry on downhill. About 250 yds past the end of the wood, look out for a small stile on the right (it is just before an electricity pole and there are two wooden gates opposite each other) ❷. Cross the stile and keep to the left of the field, curving to the left. Go through the gate at the bottom and straight ahead past the two oak trees in the next field to a metal gate. Bear left in the next field, reach the stone stile in the left corner and turn right onto Highlightley Lane.

Turn left after only 40 yds. There is a footpath sign, but it is obscured by vegetation in summer. Go through a narrow band of trees, cross the stone stile and proceed ahead, keeping to the left of the field to another stile. Cross the stone bridge and go along the unmade lane, before emerging onto Bradley Lane (B6051 Millthorpe - Barlow road) ❸.

Take the path opposite and follow this uphill, across four fields. In the fifth field, stay close to the woodland to your right and at the far corner of the field follow the path left, over the crest of the hill and onto Far Lane ❹.

Turn right along the lane as far as the farm. Bear right (signposted), through the farmyard and then follow the track downhill all the way to the woods ahead (just under a quarter of a mile). Follow the path into and through the wood, emerging into farmland after about 100 yds. Make for the farm ahead, cross the stile, turn right for 20 yds then take the lane between the farmhouse and the farm buildings. At the gate, if very wet, go through the gate and downhill on the path through the fields, but otherwise continue down the covered lane to the left of the gate. At the bottom, cross the stream and continue up the lane (the path through the fields rejoins here), until the lane widens out. Cross the ford, and eventually reach the centre of Millthorpe, where the Royal Oak is situated. ➎

Cross the road and head up Millthorpe Lane opposite. After about 200 yds and on the bend, take the path on the left at the signpost. Don't follow the bridleway, but cross the stile at the gate (marked with a yellow arrow) and follow uphill. It can be extremely muddy here, as cattle congregate near the stream. Keep the stream just to your left and climb for about 250 yds. There is a footbridge on the left beyond a boggy patch and which you will have to look out for. Cross this and emerge into a field. Keep to the right and reach a stile at the top. Continue to climb up through the second field. Take the stile on the right about 50 yds below the top of the second field. Follow the path steeply uphill a short distance, onto a muddy lane and emerge at the top of Millthorpe Lane. Turn left and, after a few yards, reach your starting point.

Places of Interest

Cartledge Hall - (Please see the previous chapter for the early history of Cartledge Hall.) As noted in the previous chapter, Cartledge Hall has a splendid interior, with fine plaster moulded ceilings, and oak panelled walls. The master bedroom has a fine barrel-vaulted ceiling. One of the most unusual features is a "water clock", although only the casing survives and none of the mechanism. It is believed that the "clock" could have been a sham to hide the priest's hole above. However, if the clock was genuine, the mechanism would have been powered by water falling onto it at 60 drops a minute.

From at least the 19th century, the house was let out to tenants and gradually decayed. In 1875, one tenant farmer, a Mark Spittlehouse, supposedly kept his fowls in the master bedroom!

View across Cordwell Valley from below Cartledge

From 1892, the Gilchrist family lived at Cartledge Hall. Mr Murray
Gilchrist was a gifted preacher, Mrs Gilchrist and their two daughters were
all successful authors, but it was their son, Robert Murray Gilchrist, who
was the most well-known of them all at the time. He was a prolific and
talented writer of novels and short stories. He died at an early age in 1917,
but his sisters continued to live in the house until they each died. After the
Second World War, the house was virtually derelict and came close to
being pulled down. Fortunately, it was acquired and restored to good
order by the late Basil Doncaster.

Great Brindwood - 'Brindwood' means 'burnt wood', which gives a clue to the charcoal burning which took place here. Charcoal was used to smelt lead. Lead smelting generally took place on exposed hilltops, known as 'boles', which helped to dissipate the dreadful fumes which were produced by the process. There are many hilltops marked 'Bolehill' on today's OS maps, which are testament to an industry which existed from Roman times until the 19th century.

Millthorpe - The name literally means "mill hamlet". There was a mill at Millthorpe until 1971, when it was demolished. There had been a mill next to Cordwell Brook since pre-Norman times, when this was the 'Lord's Mill' and all tenants of the Lord of the Manor were obliged to grind their corn here. Not only that, but they had to take their bread to be baked at the Lord's bakehouse at Cartledge and they could only buy beer from the Lord's brewhouse (situated next to the churchyard in Holmesfield, where the Angel pub is today)!

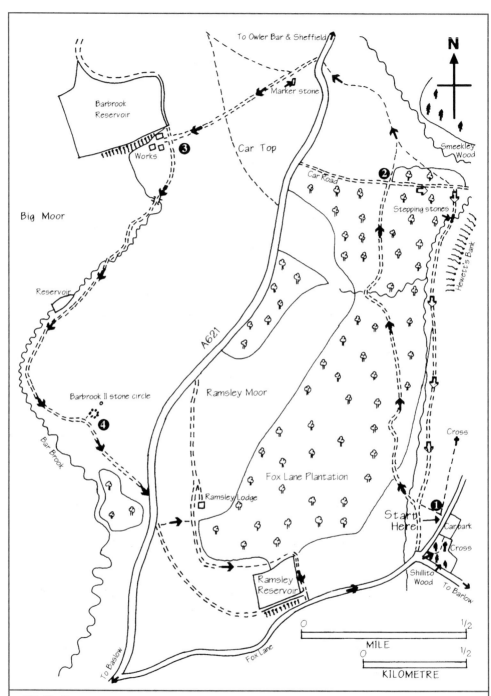

Walk 6 Shillito Wood - Fox Lane Plantation - Barbrook Reservoir - Bar Brook Stone Circle - Ramsley Reservoir - Shillito Wood.

Route: Shillito Wood - Fox Lane Plantation - Barbrook Reservoir - Bar Brook Stone Circle - Ramsley Reservoir - Shillito Wood.

Approximate distance: 5.25 miles (8 km)

Starting point: Shillito Wood car park.

Map reference: SK295750.

Required maps: OS Outdoor Leisure 24 (The White Peak) - 1:25,000 scale. Alternatively, Landranger 119 (Buxton, Matlock and Dovedale) - 1:50,000 scale.

Terrain: Open moorland, woodland on easy paths. Some uphill stretches. Not recommended in severe weather. Stone circle.

Refreshments: None.

Approximate time: 2 hours 20 minutes

Public transport: None.

The Walk

The walk starts from the Shillito Wood car park on Fox Lane ❶, which in itself is a good spot for a picnic. Shillito Wood is relatively small, but is worth exploring and has a stone cross, which is only 50 yds from the car park.

From the car park, cross Fox Lane and go through the gate in the drystone wall. Head downhill for about 50 yds and join the further of the two tracks which meet here and follow downhill by bearing right. Stay on the track for about a mile as it meanders downhill across moorland, and then through woodland.

Eventually reach a gate and crossroads ❷, where you continue ahead on a path that climbs gradually and curves left, through bracken and past a

Barbrook Stone Circle

diversity of trees and moorland plants. There is a good view of Smeekley Wood on the right and a glimpse of the Cordwell valley beyond the trees.

Reach and cross the main road, and go through the white gate and along the water company track (concessionary path). After about 200 yds you will come across a standing stone, which is an old signpost pointing the way to Sheffield on one side and Chesterfield on the other. Continue along the track towards the reservoir and buildings. Just before the buildings, bear left on the track signposted "Barbrook Valley" and "Beware Adders" ❸.

Follow the track downhill through the valley, passing a smaller reservoir (which is a haven for ducks and other water fowl) and a prehistoric stone circle ❹ (on the left after a mile and a third). There are extensive moorland views, particularly near the stone circle.

At the main road, cross and climb the stile next to the white gates leading onto the track. Here, if you wish, you can simply follow the track for half a mile and pass to the right of Ramsley Reservoir. To gain a better view, however, turn left immediately after the gate and climb steeply until a grassy road is reached. Turn right and follow around the fringe of Fox Lane Plantation to Ramsley Reservoir, passing to the left of the reservoir over boggy ground, turning right at the end of the reservoir and making for Fox Lane.

On the lane, turn left and walk the third of a mile to Shillito Wood, diverting if you wish through the wood to the stone cross, or alternatively proceeding straight back to the car park.

Optional shorter walk (3.5 km - 2.25 miles)

Start the walk as described above, except when the gate is reached after a mile, turn right, heading down the stony lane. After about 300 yds, turn right through the gate and follow the track towards a stream. Use the stepping stones to cross the stream. If you fancy a picnic or a rest, just before the stones, there is a flat grassy area to the right, which is a good place to sit on a dry day.

Cross the stream and continue along the track uphill for about a mile, until you reach the path on the left, which returns you to the car park.

Places of Interest

Marker Stones - There are three marker stones passed by on this walk. The first is visible at the start of the walk on the right as you descend from Fox Lane. Along with the stone in Shillito Wood, this is an ecclesiastical stone and would have been erected by the monastery at Beauchief Abbey, which at one time held the land in this area. They both guide the way and act as boundary markers. The cross in Shillito Wood is the better preserved. The third marker is located on the track to Barbrook Reservoir. This is a true directional marker, saying "Sheffield Way" on one side

Marker Stone

Stone Cross in Shillito Wood

and "Chesterfield Way" on the other. It should be borne in mind that before the advent of good roads, the crossing of the higher moors was a hazardous business on boggy and rough tracks. The marker stones acted as essential aids to navigation in otherwise featureless landscapes.

Barbrook II Stone Circle and other prehistoric remains - Barbrook II stone circle is one of the best preserved in Derbyshire. It dates from at least 1500 BC. There is a ring of 12 stones plus several outlying stones. The stones are aligned to events such as Midsummer, Midwinter, and the Vernal and Autumnal Equinoxes, for sunsets and sunrises. They are aligned with astonishing accuracy, given the crude technology available to their builders. Near to the circle is a stone cairn, which could have been a burial chamber. No human remains have been discovered, but the soil is very acidic and such remains are unlikely to be preserved for several thousand years in these conditions. There are other stone circles on Big Moor, but this is the most visible.

On the moorland on the west side of Bar Brook, there is an area known as Swine Sty. Here there are the earliest known signs of Bronze Age settlement (with the exception of cave dwellings) in the Peak District. Stone foundations, hut circles, pottery, and flint, bone and stone tools have all been unearthed. There is evidence of the pasturing of animals and primitive agriculture.

Fox Lane - This is named after a local family, who were prominent in the 15th and 16th centuries. Fox Lane stretches from the Cordwell valley to the A621 Owler Bar to Baslow road.

Shillito Wood - In the past, the wood was used for "coaling", that is charcoal burning. Nearby, there are the remains of bolehills, where lead smelting was carried out. In 1570, men working here noticed a long line of riders in the distance, climbing from Baslow and heading for Totley Moor. They were to learn that it was Mary Queen of Scots, being taken from Chatsworth House to incarceration in Sheffield Castle.

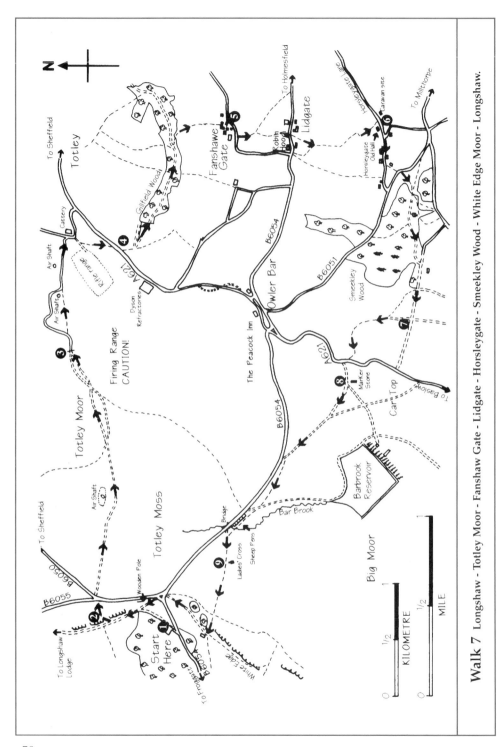

Walk 7 Longshaw - Totley Moor - Fanshaw Gate - Lidgate - Horsleygate - Smeekley Wood - White Edge Moor - Longshaw.

Route: Longshaw - Totley Moor - Fanshaw Gate - Lidgate - Horsleygate - Smeekley Wood - White Edge Moor - Longshaw.

Approximate distance: 10.5 miles (17 km)

Starting point: Car park near Wooden Pole, Longshaw Country Park

Map reference: SK267789.

Required maps: OS Outdoor Leisure 24 (The White Peak) - 1:25,000 scale or Landranger 119 (Buxton, Matlock and Dovedale) - 1:50,000 scale.

Terrain: A long walk, so plenty of stamina is required. Moorland, woodland and farmland. Mainly on good tracks, but some are hard to follow in poor weather conditions.

Refreshments: The Robin Hood, Lidgate. National Trust café at Longshaw Lodge (this is slightly off the route).

Approximate time: 5 hours.

Public transport: Buses from Sheffield to the Fox House, which is about half a mile from the start of this walk.

The Walk

The walk starts from the National Trust car park ❶ at the southern end of the Longshaw Estate, which is on the Froggatt road (B6054) about 250 yds from the junction with the Owler Bar - Fox House road (B6054/B6055).

Just outside the eastern boundary wall of the car park there is a broad grassy track that joins another track and goes northwards in the direction of Longshaw Lodge. Follow this track, until reaching stone steps which climb up the crags to the right ❷. At the top, there is a wide vista across Longshaw, along the Hope Valley and beyond. From here, follow a path that leads to the Fox House road (B6055) behind the crags. The road at this point splits into two, so cross both roads to the gate opposite.

Follow the track straight ahead across Totley Moor towards the railway air shaft, which dominates the sombre landscape. The path is fairly flat and without difficulty, if somewhat monotonous, but it is well worth persevering for the views up ahead. After about two thirds of a mile, pass the air shaft and take note of the danger signs to your right. These warn you not to cross the moors to the right when firing practice is taking place (red flags or lights will be shown), but as long as you keep to the track all will be fine, even if the military are practising. Keep going for another two thirds of a mile and begin to descend. Eventually you will be rewarded with an excellent view of Sheffield, Rotherham and beyond.

The path drops more steeply and winds downhill to a gate ❸, where the track becomes a lane. As the lane curves left, take the stile on the right over the wire fence and head downhill across a couple of fields towards another air shaft (you can alternatively stay on the lane). After passing the shaft, rejoin the lane (which is now surfaced) and head downhill past a few houses to reach an oblique T-junction (with a cattery opposite). Turn right and continue downhill, turning right again onto an unsurfaced lane after about 75 yds. Follow this lane a short way, cross a stream that flows across the lane and climb over the stone stile to your left. Follow the path diagonally uphill (waymarked) until the main road (A621) is reached. Turn right along the road for about 100 yds, then cross over and take the path on the left ❹.

Cross the field to a stile, then take the path which runs just to the right of the coniferous trees (don't cross the second stile, or take the track sharp left). Follow the path between the trees and the fence until reaching the wood up ahead. Stay on the broad track for about half a mile as it winds through the wood. Eventually, the path curves left, is partly shored up by logs and the wood falls away steeply to the right and down to a stream. Shortly after this, take the right hand fork down to the white timber footbridge. Emerge from the wood and head straight ahead uphill through a narrow field with several trees and bushes in it. Keep to the right in the second and third fields and then cross the stile just left of the large stone barn. Turn left on the driveway and right onto Fanshaw Gate Lane ❺.

Fanshawe Gate Hall

Continue up the lane for about 100 yds, past Fanshaw Gate Hall, then turn left at the signposted footpath. Climb for about 150 yds and take the right hand path at the signpost, keeping to the right of the field and parallel with the electricity lines. Eventually, emerge onto the road. At this point either cross over to the signposted footpath opposite, or walk along the road about 150 yds to the Robin Hood pub for some food and refreshment.

Once on the path opposite, cross the wire fence at the stile provided (NB this fence may not be a permanent feature) and then cross the second stile ahead and proceed straight ahead across the field. Go through a large metal gate and continue downhill. At the end of the field, the path turns 90° to the right for 40 yds and then back downhill. Cross another field, passing behind the tennis court of Old Horsleygate Hall, and emerge onto Horsleygate Lane ❻.

Turn right onto the lane and follow it downhill for about quarter of a mile, taking the signposted path left which is just after a modern barn and passes just right of a modern bungalow-cum-stable block ("Bonny Brook") and between fences. On reaching the road, climb the partially obscured

Lodge near White Edge

stile opposite and follow the indistinct path, which gradually curves right and joins a broader path. Follow this into Smeekley Wood and keep going ahead, ignoring paths off to both sides. After about a third of a mile the track joins a straight bridle road (signposted "Baslow Road"). Turn right onto this and continue ahead, past Smeekley Farm, climbing on a stony surface with woodland either side. When the woodland ends, you reach a cross roads ❼.

Turn right through the stone gate posts onto a path that climbs gradually and curves left. There is a good view of Smeekley Wood to the right as well as a glimpse of the Cordwell valley beyond the trees. The path reaches the main road (A621), which you cross, before going through the gate and along the water company track (concessionary path). After about 200 yds reach a marker stone ❽, which is a signpost pointing the way to Sheffield on one side and Chesterfield on the other. Bear right on the broad, grassy track and climb gradually.

The track eventually reaches the B6054 at a gate, but take the smaller path just to the left and follow the small waymark posts with white arrows.

After about a quarter of a mile the path joins a wider track, which leads from Barbrook Reservoir to the road. Bear right onto this very briefly, then left on the smaller path (still waymarked), passing to the left of some sheep pens which are up against the stone wall adjacent to the road. Cross the stream (Bar Brook) and then take the signposted path diagonally left and uphill. This path is narrower than a track just to the left of it, but is waymarked. In poor weather conditions this path is hard to follow, as the landscape is relatively featureless.

After about 200 yds you can take a slight diversion to the remains of Ladies' Cross ❾, of which on a stump is still standing, although the rest is on the ground nearby. Rejoin the track and head for the small wooden marker on the crest. Continue up as the path begins to level and reveals extensive views of the Dark Peak, including Mam Tor and Kinder Scout. Eventually you will reach a stile and a post and wire fence. Go down through the gap towards the lodge house. Just before reaching it, bear right onto a stone track and continue until reaching the road. Cross the triangular road island and head towards the white gate and the Wooden Pole. Once through the gate, take the broad, grassy track slightly downhill for 75 yds. Then turn left onto a similar track and back towards the car park.

Wooden Pole near Longshaw

Places of Interest

Longshaw - Longshaw Lodge was built by the Duke of Rutland as a shooting lodge for hunting parties in the late 19th century. The estate was purchased by the National Trust in 1973. The Lodge itself is now divided into private apartments, but the public are free to wander around the estate. There are tearooms near to the Lodge, an ornamental lake and good views in most directions. Every September, the Longshaw Sheepdog Trials are held here.

Totley Tunnel - At the time that the tunnel was completed in 1892, it was the longest railway tunnel in the world, running beneath Totley Moor between Grindleford and Totley Brook for 6230 yds. Even today, it is the second longest tunnel in Britain (ignoring the Channel Tunnel). It has only four air vents, three of them at the Totley Brook end and one large vent in the middle of Totley Moor. This is because the Duke of Rutland opposed the building of the tunnel, which passed beneath his estate, and was able to stipulate that only one air shaft could be built on his land.

Fanshaw Gate Hall - Behind the rather grand gateposts, the hall is a fraction of its original size, as it was partly dismantled in the 17th century when the Fanshawe family moved along the lane to Woodthorpe Hall. The large stone barn was originally the tithe barn and dates from the 16th century. The house is not open to the public, but usually there is an open weekend during the summer, when the public can view the garden.

Horsleygate Lane - The lane is thought to be named after Adam de Horsley who lived in the vicinity in the 14th century. The suffix '-gate' has the same meaning as 'way' or 'street' throughout Northern England and is a word of Norse origin ('gata'), although in some instances does mean 'entrance' (Norse word 'geat').

Smeekley Wood - The name is derived from 'smeclif', which means 'smooth, steep slope'.

Ladies Cross - This stone cross, which is partly demolished, was erected by the monks of Beauchief Abbey, probably serving the dual purpose of marking their boundary and pointing the way for travellers. The cross also marked the intersection of the boundaries of the parishes of Hathersage, Holmesfield and Totley, although the modern boundaries are now a little different. The base bears the inscription "MB + †IR 1618". The cross is a Grade II listed building.

Ladies Cross

Wooden Pole - This marks the junction between the Owler Bar - Fox House road and the road from Stoney Middleton and Froggatt and is a landmark in a featureless landscape. Before the advent of surfaced roads, widespread use of maps and road signs, such navigational aids were vital. This is not the original pole, but a pole will have stood on this spot for centuries. There is a similar pole between Stanage Edge and Redmires which serves the same purpose.

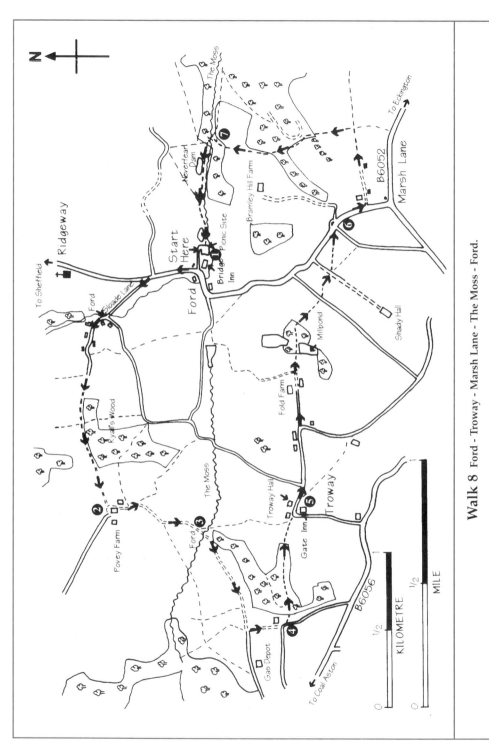

Walk 8 Ford - Troway - Marsh Lane - The Moss - Ford.

Route: Ford - Troway - Marsh Lane - The Moss - Ford.

Approximate distance: 5.6 miles (9 km)

Starting point: Ford picnic site, midway between Marsh Lane and Ridgeway, near the Bridge Inn.

Map reference: SK403804.

Required maps: Pathfinders 743, 744 761, and 762 - 1:25,000 scale. Alternatively, Landrangers 110, 119 and 120 - 1:50,000 scale.

Terrain: Woodland, farmland, mainly good paths and tracks. Easy going, some very short climbs.

Refreshments: Bridge Inn, Ford; Gate Inn, Troway

Approximate time: 3 hours.

Public transport: Buses from Sheffield, Crystal Peaks, Eckington and Chesterfield.

The Walk

The walk starts at the picnic site beside the Bridge Inn at Ford ❶ between the villages of Marsh Lane and Ridgeway, and makes a circuit which centres on The Moss valley. The walk can be adapted quite easily to make it shorter or longer as desired. The only problem arises with the Ordnance Survey maps, as this area is spread across no fewer than four 1:25,000 Pathfinder maps and three 1:50,000 Landranger maps.

From the picnic site, walk back to the road, turn right and head uphill for almost a quarter of a mile. Turn left onto Sloade Lane, and follow it down to a ford. Continue ahead along the lane past several large houses and cottages. The lane then becomes muddier and passes to the right of Ryall's Wood. Follow the path downhill and then uphill again, heading towards Povey Farm on the hilltop ❷.

At the gate near the farm, turn left down the lane between farm buildings and follow as it winds its way downhill to The Moss in the valley bottom. Use the footbridge to avoid the muddy ford over The Moss ❸, but ignore the footpath that goes off left (unless you wish to take a shortcut up to Troway).

Continue as the lane climbs and begins to narrow. In summer, the thick growth of brambles can make it difficult to get through, but after a while, the lane widens again. About half a mile after the footbridge, take the 90° left hand turn and follow the lane towards Sicklebrook Farm ❹.

As you pass the farm buildings, another lane joins at a sharp bend, but continue ahead and slightly uphill for about 75 yds, before crossing the somewhat obscured stile on the left. Drop steeply across the small field, over a stile and into the wood. Then follow the broad track through pleasant woodland to the gate at the far end. Continue along the track across the field to a stile in the far right hand corner. Follow the narrow passage to the road, emerging opposite the Gate Inn, which is a convenient stopping place ❺.

Follow the road past Troway Hall and through the village of Troway for about a third of a mile. The road then turns sharp right, but continue straight ahead along the track past Great Fold Farm and Fold Farm eventually crossing a stile. Then descend down a path between a hedge and a wire fence to the trees at the valley bottom. Continue across the millpond wall (the pond is now a fishing lake) and diagonally uphill through the trees at the far side.

Emerge into a field and follow the path directly ahead uphill to the top, where there is a stile and gate. Turn left onto the lane very briefly, then cross the stile on your right. Go diagonally left across the field to the stile and then follow the right hand side of the next field until reaching a lane with a stile next to the gate opposite. Head diagonally left and uphill on an indistinct path across the field. The top corner will initially be out of sight, but once there, cross the stile and emerge onto a main road ❻.

Cross over the road and turn right along it for about 200 yds, before turning left down through a farmyard. Go through a gate, and follow the green lane uphill for 200 yds to a stile at the end. Keep to the right across the field reaching a metal gate. Immediately turn left and follow the hedge towards the wood. Cross the wooden fence-cum-stile into the wood and follow the path ahead and downhill, briefly emerging into a field and then passing back into the wood.

Continue ahead on the path and climb uphill with saplings to your right. Pass over the crest of the hill and drop downhill, emerging into the right hand corner of a field. Keep going through a small wood and then descend through more two fields before reaching another wood. At the valley bottom, cross the white footbridge and bear left ❼.

Follow the broad track along the left hand side of the first fishing pond, known as Neverfear Dam, and continue to the far end of the field. Bear right through the gap stile and follow the fenced path to the next stile on the left. Continue across several fields and through the picnic/recreation area. Keep to the left of the second fishing pond and reach the car park.

View across the Moss Valley

A farmhouse at Ford.

Places of Interest

Ford - The hamlet of Ford was at the heart of the ancient forest of the Manor of Eckington. It was a well-stocked hunting ground and was consequently tempting to poachers, who would raid the fallow deer. If the culprits were not caught or found they were declared "outlaws". One such outlaw was Robin Hood. It is not terribly surprising that it is said that Ford was a haunt for Robin and his merry men, as Ford is fairly close to Sherwood Forest and Little John reputedly hailed from Hathersage about twelve miles away. The Sitwells of Renishaw Hall (only about three miles away) have a long bow which is supposed to have been Robin Hood's.

Ridgeway - A place of interest near to Ford (although not on the route of the walk), is Ridgeway, which straddles the ridge above the Moss Valley. In the days before good roads and drainage, the ridge from Gleadless down to Eckington was a major thoroughfare from Sheffield and the Peak, as lower lying ground was prone to flooding. Today, a former farm converted into the Ridgeway Cottage Industry Centre is an interesting place to visit. It is open all year from 10.30 am to 5.00 pm Tuesday - Sunday, plus Bank Holiday Mondays.

Troway - The unusual name for the village literally means 'trough or valley road' (derived from 'trogweg'), although the village and road are actually above the valley bottom.

Troway Hall - This fine 17th century farmhouse is a Grade II listed building with some more modern additions. Nearby Troway Hall Farm also has an interesting stone frontage.

The Sickle and Scythe Industry in the Moss Valley - On the route of this walk, there are a few remnants of the industry which thrived in this area from about 1500 until the industrial revolution and the introduction of the factory system. There are various old millponds, now mostly used by anglers. These are at Ford, Neverfear Dam, and close to Fold Farm. Some of the place names, such as Sicklebrook Farm, allude to the industrial past of the valley.

Gate Inn, Troway

63

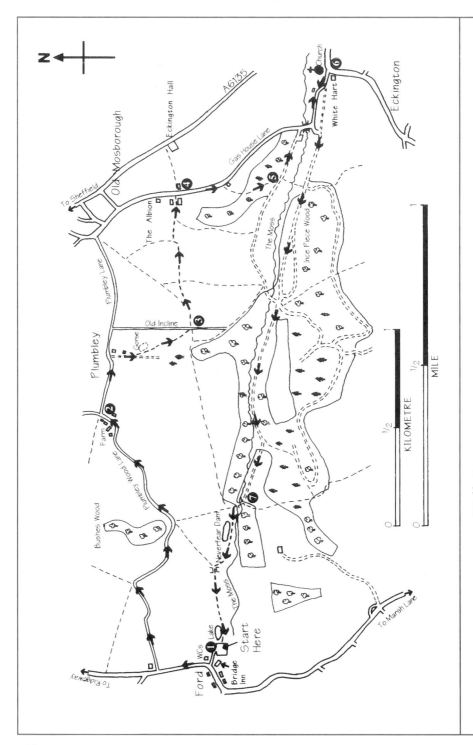

Walk 9 Ford - Troway - Marsh Lane - The Moss - Ford.

> **Route:** Ford - Plumbley - Eckington - The Moss - Ford
>
> **Approximate distance:** 5 miles (8 km)
>
> **Starting point:** Ford picnic site, midway between Marsh Lane and Ridgeway, near Bridge Inn.
>
> **Map reference:** SK403804.
>
> **Required maps:** Pathfinder 744 and 762 - 1:25,000 scale. Alternatively, Landranger 120 - 1:50,000 scale.
>
> **Terrain:** Farmland and woodland, mainly on lanes and easy tracks.
>
> **Refreshments:** Bridge Inn, Ford; The Albion, Plumbley/Mosborough; The White Hart, Eckington
>
> **Approximate time:** 2 hours 30 minutes
>
> **Public transport:** Buses from Sheffield, Crystal Peaks, Eckington and Chesterfield.

The Walk

The walk starts at the picnic site beside the Bridge Inn at Ford ❶ between the villages of Marsh Lane and Ridgeway, and makes a circuit which centres on The Moss valley.

From the car park, head back towards the road and turn right and walk uphill for about 300 yds. Turn right onto the lane, which is signposted "No Vehicles, Bridle Path Only" and continue along this lane with fields on either side. After about quarter of a mile, the lane swings to the left and drops downhill, before turning sharp right. Ignore all other paths and stay on the lane, which climbs gradually past a wooded knoll on the left. Continue over the top of the hill and head for the farm up ahead with good views across the Moss valley. At the farm, the lane passes a number of farm buildings and several cottages, before coming to a junction ❷.

Turn right (blue waymark) onto another lane and drop slightly downhill for about 200 yds, before turning right again at a stile in front of a stone cottage and a bungalow (yellow waymark). Follow the track across the field. As you pass gorse bushes on your left, strike slightly left and uphill towards a stile. In the next field, strike diagonally left and downhill (the path is obvious when no crop is growing). At the far end of the field cross over what seems to be a straight and sunken lane, but which is actually an old incline that was used for hauling coal from the valley bottom up to Plumbley ❸.

Take the path opposite and follow across an open field and after a short distance to the left of a hedge. There is a view of Eckington church over to the right. Keep on ahead, stay close to the hedge and ignore the path to the right after about 300 yds. After passing over a slight crest, continue down to the far end of the field and turn left for 30 yds before crossing a stile.

Go straight across the narrow field that you find yourself in. Cross two sets of stiles and pass through a narrow band of trees, before heading steeply uphill towards the stone buildings at the top. Cross a stone stile between

View across The Moss Valley from Plumbley Wood Lane

two stone buildings and follow
the lane towards the road ❹.
Here there is a pub ("The
Albion") a short way left, but
otherwise turn right and follow
the road past several cottages
and downhill. There is an
excellent view across Eckington
towards Renishaw Hall and Park.

Follow the road (Gas House
Lane) until reaching a red metal
gate on the right, just before a
Severn Trent Water pumping
station. Pass through the gate
and cross the field towards the

The Bridge Inn, Ford

wood ahead. The path enters the wood and drops downhill past several
holly bushes before dropping more steeply. At the bottom ❺, reach a broad
track and turn left onto it. Stay on this track until reaching a car park,
which you pass through before bearing right onto a lane (Gas House Lane
again). Follow this over a small bridge across The Moss and then right
towards a white barrier. (At this point you can instead stay on the lane,
which bears left, and follow this as far as SS Peter and Paul Church, which
has a squat broach spire, or to The White Hart pub, returning the way you
have come) ❻.

Once through the white barrier, follow the track uphill for 50m then bear
right onto another track and proceed towards the woodland ahead. Stay
on the broad track that keeps to the valley bottom and fairly close to The
Moss, passing through beech and oak woodland. Along the way, there are
remains of former mining activities, including an old pithead building and
a small overgrown spoil heap. Although mining was carried out as
recently as this century, nature is once again reclaiming the valley and it is
hard to believe this was once a hive of industry. Stay on the track for about
a mile. Eventually, the woodland opens out with a field on the left hand
side. Shortly afterwards reach a white footbridge ❼.

Cross the footbridge and follow the broad track passing to the left of the
first fishing pond (called "Neverfear Dam"), and continue to the narrow
end of the field. Bear right through the stile and follow the fenced path to

the next stile, then bear left across a field to another stile. Finish the walk by passing through the picnic/recreation area and to the left of the second fishing pond back to the car park.

Places of Interest

Ford Dam - There used to be a grinding house and turning shop here, although the dam is used purely by anglers today.

Old Incline - The incline now just looks like a straight, but steep, lane. In the late 19th and early 20th century, it was used as a tramway for hauling coal up from the valley bottom to the coke ovens at Plumbley.

Renishaw Hall and Park - (Not on the route of the walk) For about 400 years this has been the family seat of the Sitwells, best known in the 20th century for the literary trio of Edith, Osbert and Sacheverell. The house was built in about 1625 and was enlarged between 1793 and 1808 by Joseph Badger of Sheffield. In 1908, the house was remodelled by Sir Edwin Luytens. The 4 acre Italian gardens are open to the public from Easter to September on Friday, Saturday, Sunday and Bank Holidays. There is also a museum and art gallery.

Eckington - Eckington was first mentioned in documents in 1002. Although agriculture dominated for many centuries, the presence of coal seams led to the growth of the mining industry, upon which the village was dependent until very recently. The last pit in North East Derbyshire, at Renishaw, closed in 1989.

Parish Church - The parish church of St Peter and St Paul is one of the most elegant 12th and 13th century churches in Derbyshire. Within the church there are monuments to several members of the Sitwell family.

Industry in the Moss Valley - As early as 1386, the Abbot of Wellbeck contracted William Mason of Mosborough to build an iron furnace in the forest half a mile east of Ford. The iron was extracted by burning rock with charcoal and the impurities had to be beaten out, as the temperature was insufficient to make the iron a fluid. By Tudor times, however, water powered blast furnaces had been invented, that increased the heat of the fire somewhat.

By the late 15th century, an increasing number of trees had been felled to provide charcoal, which led to more land being cultivated. This in turn increased demand for new tools to reap the crops and caused more water mills to be built to grind corn. The persistent wars with Spain in the 15th and 16th centuries also caused many oak trees to be felled for shipbuilding, changing the heavily wooded landscape into the familiar patchwork landscape we know today. The increased demand for tools and the realisation that crops could be grown for profit led to the development of the sickle and scythe industry around the Moss Valley, which thrived until the industrial revolution.

In the 19th century and until quite recently, the coal industry was dominant in the area around Eckington. Within the woods to the west of Eckington, and along the route of this walk, there were some small scale mining operations, the remains of which can still be seen today in the form of a small overgrown slagheap and ruined pithead buildings.

Neverfear Dam - Although now a fishing lake, there is documentary evidence of an ancient dam and a medieval iron furnace at this location. In the 1850s there was a grinding wheel housed in a building. The large blocks of stone near one end of the dam could be the remains of the mill.

Old Mine Buildings

Walk 10 Middle Handley - West Handley - Grasscroft Wood - Hundall - Middle Handley

Route: Middle Handley - West Handley - Grasscroft Wood - Hundall - Middle Handley

Approximate distance: 4 miles (6.5 km)

Starting point: Middle Handley outside Devonshire Arms.

Map reference: SK404778

Required maps: Pathfinders 761 and 762 - 1:25,000 scale. Alternatively, Landrangers 119 and 120 - 1:50,000 scale.

Terrain: Farmland, woodland, open views, easy going.

Refreshments: The Miners Arms, Hundall. Devonshire Arms, Middle Handley.

Approximate time: 2 hours.

Public transport: Buses from Chesterfield, Eckington and Sheffield.

The Walk

The walk starts in the hamlet of Middle Handley, about one mile south west of Eckington. Park on Westfield Lane near the Devonshire Arms pub. ❶ Middle Handley like most of the places on this walk, is a quiet backwater tucked into the hinterland between Whittington, Eckington and Unstone.

Leave the hamlet along Westfield Lane heading west. Just before the national speed limit sign, take the signposted path on the left, and strike out diagonally across the field, which is known locally as 'The Murder Field', after the brutal murder of Eliza Hudson by her husband in 1873. Pass through the hedgerow and keep to the left of the next field for about 75 yds, then strike out on the path diagonally right (in summer there may be a tall crop, but the path is quite broad). At the far side, pass through a gap next to a short section of drystone wall and follow the path along the

West Handley

left of the next field to a stile, through a paddock and to the left of the larger farm buildings ❷.

Emerge onto the lane in West Handley (a hamlet that is pleasant and unspoiled) and bear left, following the lane past a converted chapel (now a house) and to the T-junction. Turn left and follow the road for 200 yds, cross over near the crest and take the path opposite, by passing through the gap next to the metal gate. Follow the path downhill towards the houses and the white lamp post. Cross over the lane near the houses and take the path opposite climbing up through the trees. The path is fairly broad and winds uphill through trees, which gradually thin out and are replaced by gorse bushes. As you climb, pass the remains of some old brick buildings and reach a timber stile. Ignore the path that goes off to the left and proceed directly towards Grasscroft Wood on the hilltop ❸.

At Grasscroft Wood, turn right and follow the path along the outside edge of the wood. After a while the telecommunications mast comes into view. Follow the path towards the mast, briefly entering the wood and then emerging back into the fields. At the lane turn right for 50 yds or so, then take the signposted path on the left ❹.

Follow the path along the hilltop, with open views to either side, and keep close to the right hand boundary until the path starts to descend more steeply. Head towards Ramshaw Wood, which is directly ahead, bearing right just in front of the wood. The path drops down to the corner of the field and into the wood. It then descends and broadens into a wide track. Stay on the track as it levels out and begins to climb again. The track leaves the wood and then becomes a surfaced lane. Continue past Woodsmithies Farm and eventually climb up to a T-junction. Turn right and follow the road uphill into Hundall, where the Miner's Arms pub is a possible refreshment stop. Alternatively, there is a handy bench for a sandwich stop ❺.

Turn left at the junction and follow the road for 200 yds with good views to the left, turning right at the footpath signpost. Follow the track past a bungalow, directly in front of an ivy clad cottage and then through a small gate. Ignore the path to the right and continue ahead across the field towards Stubbing Wood. At the wood you can take a diversion to explore the network of paths within the wood, but this walk takes the path that just passes briefly through the left corner and back out into the fields ❻.

Follow the path across two fields towards the road and cross over, taking the path opposite that crosses diagonally left and slightly uphill towards Ash Lane. Turn right onto the lane and follow past Ash Lane Farm, with its thatched roof, and reach a T-junction. Take the footpath opposite and follow directly ahead across several fields back to Westfield Lane. Bear right and follow back to your starting point.

Places of Interest

Middle and West Handley - The name 'Handley' means 'at the high clearing'.

Devonshire Arms - The name bears witness to the landownership in the area in the past, as the village formed part of the Duke of Devonshire's estate.

The Murder Field - The first field crossed on this walk bears this name because of a brutal murder that occurred on 24th April 1873. Benjamin Hudson clubbed his wife, Eliza, to death near the stile. They were estranged and he had spotted her walking across the field. They had

Devonshire Arms, Middle Handley

words that led to his savage attack. An inquest was held in the Church School and a post mortem at the Devonshire Arms. The accused did not attend the inquest, which was fortunate as there was a lynch mob out to get him. The murder aroused much local curiosity and over one thousand people came to pay their respects to the laid out corpse. Eventually, Ben Hudson was sent for trial at Derby Assizes, where he was found guilty of murder and was sentenced to be hanged. A last minute appeal was unsuccessful and he was hanged on 4th August 1873. This was the first private hanging at Derby Gaol, all previous hangings having been in public. The whole affair attracted much media attention, some of which was lurid in the extreme! An excellent account of this case can be found in Amos Ford's booklet "A Trilogy of Murder".

Hundall - The name 'Hundall' is thought to mean 'Dog's Hill'. In the 17th century, the area was referred to as 'Hundall Pits', which suggests that a good deal of mining was taking place at the time. The oldest farm in the village is thought to be Hall Farm, which was owned in the 17th century by the Chantrey family, who were yeoman freeholders. Manor Farm, near the Miners' Arms, was never part of the Manor of Unstone, so it is unclear why it bears the name.

Mining - There is still evidence of mining in the disturbed ground opposite the Miners' Arms. Throughout the mining areas of North East Derbyshire, mining would have taken place initially near the surface in the form of 'bell pits'. Eventually, drift mines were sunk, which were able to exploit seams of coal further below ground. It was only in the 19th century that deep shafts were sunk.

N

BARLOW

Church
Tearooms
The Peacock
5

Farm
Newgate
4

Three
Merry
Lads
Methodist
Chapel

CUTTHORPE

B6051

To Whittington Moor

Four Lanes End

To Chesterfield

Cutthorpe Hall

House
with pool

Oxton Rakes

The
Gate
3

To Baslow

B6050

Pratthall

School

Kitchenflat/
Wood

Start

WCs

Lower
Reservoir

1

Middle
Reservoir

Upper
Reservoir

2

Linacre Woods

To Baslow

KILOMETRE
0   ½   1

MILE
0   ½

Walk 11 Linacre Woods - Oxton Rakes - Barlow - Cutthorpe - Linacre Woods

Route: Linacre Woods - Oxton Rakes - Barlow - Cutthorpe - Linacre Woods

Approximate distance: 5.5 miles (8.75 km)

Starting point: Linacre Woods car park.

Map reference: SK336727

Required maps: Outdoor Leisure 24 (White Peak) or Pathfinder 761 (Chesterfield) both 1:25,000 scale. Alternatively, Landranger 119 (Buxton, Matlock and Dovedale) 1:50,000 scale.

Terrain: Reservoirs, woodland and farmland - opportunities for food and refreshment breaks. Steady going.

Refreshments: The Gate, Pratthall; The Peacock, Barlow; Three Merry Lads, Cutthorpe. Also, Hackney Tearooms, Barlow

Approximate time: 3 hours.

Public transport: Limited service from Chesterfield and Holmesfield to within quarter of a mile of the Linacre car parks.

The Walk

Linacre Woods are owned and managed by Severn Trent Water as a country park. This walk starts from the lower of the three visitors car parks ❶. The parks are approached from the B6050 along a single track road. There are numerous picnic places and a variety of short walks around the woods.

Take the timber steps downhill and turn right onto a broad track. Head down through the wood towards the reservoir ahead, but keep to the right hand track before reaching the reservoir. Follow the broad track for about third of a mile, i.e. the length of the reservoir, before reaching the next dam wall, where there is a viewing area on the dam wall itself ❷.

View from Oxton Rakes.

Take the path to the immediate right of the dam wall, which stays roughly parallel to the reservoir. After 300 yds, the path crosses a timber footbridge and then continues through the woods. Keep to this well-defined path for the entire length of the upper reservoir. At the far end of the reservoir, the main path crosses left on a timber footbridge and walkway; at this point, continue straight ahead rather than turning left, taking the narrow path through the trees, gradually climbing until reaching a stone wall with a timber stile. Turn right and uphill to reach a timber stile. Turn right and keep close to the stone wall for 50 yards. Then bear half left uphill (the path is indistinct) towards a gap in the band of trees near the top of the field. Behind the band of trees and in the top corner of the field, cross a stile. Then turn left and follow the wall. At the end of the field reach a muddy lane and follow it to the road. Turn right for 75 yards and then left down Oaks Lane just past "The Gate" (which serves food as well as drink) ❸.

Follow the Oaks Lane downhill towards Oxton Rakes and soak in the wonderful view of Oxton Rakes, Bolehill, Unstone and Sheffield in the far distance. At Oxton Rakes, the road turns sharp left near a house with a swimming pool in the garden. At this point leave the road and bear right along the track. After about 300 yards, the track veers left, but take instead the path across fields by crossing the low stile (watch out for stinging nettles in summer).

Cross the first field to a stile in the left corner. Pass to the right of a small stone barn and reach another stile. At this point, aim towards Newgate Farm on the hillside ahead and cross several fields. In the field immediately before the farm, follow the track almost up to the farm, but then climb uphill slightly further and go through the narrow gap beneath the sycamore trees. The path passes above the farm and emerges onto a road ❹.

Bear right along the road for about 80 yards, then turn left at the wooden signpost and go between a modern bungalow and a stone house. On reaching a field, bear half left for about 75 yards towards the solitary large tree. Go through the gap next to the gate and follow the right hand side of the next field for 100 yards. Then turn right over the stone stile and follow the path across the centre of three fields in succession, gradually losing height. Then follow the right hand side of the fourth field, cross a stile and

St. Lawrence Church, Barlow

Barlow Village

follow the path down past St Lawrence's church and churchyard to the main road. Bear right and stop for refreshments if you wish at the Hackney House Tearooms and Restaurant (meals and snacks) or The Peacock public house (drink and food) ❺.

Continue along the road for 200 yards and bear right up a track and through a five bar gate, keeping to the right until crossing the stile at the end of the field. Then keep left, cross another stile and head down towards the trees, crossing the footbridge and climbing the bank opposite. Continue up through the trees (be careful in wet conditions, as the path will be slippery). Ignore the first small path on the left (i.e. after 50 yards), but bear left at the fork after 100 yards. Continue uphill for another 100 yards before reaching a stile and entering a field. Keep to the left of the field, cross a stile and continue ahead, keeping just left of the fence. Eventually emerge onto the main road at Cutthorpe near the Methodist chapel ❻.

At the road, turn left and just after the bus stop cross over and take the path on the right across farmland reaching Cutthorpe Hall after quarter of a mile. About 50 yards before reaching the hall, cross the stile to the right (if you look up to the right, you will have a good view of Cutthorpe Old Hall about 200 yds away across the field), then keep to the left before passing through a narrow gate. Then turn left at the T-junction and pass the entrance to Cutthorpe (New) Hall. After 80 yards, turn right onto a track through trees. Cross the first small field, enter a larger field and keep to the right. Climb over a low stone stile and strike half left downhill and cross a stile into woodland about 50 yards above the bottom end of the field. Go ahead 20 yards towards a stone wall, bear left briefly, then right through a gap and, shortly afterwards, emerge into a field. Head diagonally uphill to the right and reach a lane ❼.

Turn right onto the lane and follow it into woodland. This path gradually curves left. Ignore the right fork, and emerge from the woodland, keeping to the right of the field. Halfway along the field, a path crosses at 90°. Turn left to reach the road. If you need to use toilet facilities or wish to visit the ranger station, bear left for 50 yards to the public conveniences. Otherwise, turn right up the road and return to your starting point.

Places of Interest

Linacre House - This was a fine three storey stone farmhouse, but it was demolished in the 1960s, having been vacated in 1938. It was suspected that it was polluting the lower reservoir. The house occupied the site of the present middle car park. Prior to the farmhouse being built, this was the site of Linacre Hall, ancestral home to Dr Thomas Linacre (b. 1490), first president of the Royal College of Physicians and physician to Henry VII and Henry VIII. He also taught Henry Moore and Erasmus.

The Gate - The Gate used to be known as the 'Enter Inn'. It also had the local nickname of 'The Hen Turd', because beer used to be brewed in the barn behind the pub, and hens would perch on the rafters above the fermenting beer!

Oxton Rakes - The name means 'ox or oxen paths'.

St Lawrence Church, Barlow - The church was built in about 1142. There is no aisle and no tower or steeple. The transeptal chapel was added in 1340, as a chantry chapel to the Barley family. Within it there is an alabaster tomb to Robert Barley and his wife dated 1467. Also

Cutthorpe Methodist Church

commemorated is a later Robert Barley, who died in 1532 at the age of 15, shortly after marrying Bess of Hardwick (who was even younger than him). She had a total of four husbands, built Chatsworth and is buried in grander surroundings in Derby Cathedral. The church was nearly pulled down in 1784, when George III issued a brief for demolition and rebuilding, as it was in disrepair. Insufficient funds were collected and the church was patched up. The chancel was rebuilt in 1867.

Barlow - The name either means 'boar clearing' or 'clearing where barley grows'. The manor was acquired by the d'Abitot family by marriage in 1086. In the 13th century, as was customary in those times, they took the name of the village, which at the time was known as 'Barley'. They built Barlow Hall, which was located somewhere close to the present day Hall Farm. It was demolished in about 1600 when the, by then, impoverished family could no longer afford their mortgage to Bess of Hardwick and left the area for good. The manor of Barlow later passed to the Duke of Rutland, in whose ownership it stayed until large areas of the estate were sold in 1920.

Village Water Pump and Well Dressing -The village pump was built in 1840 and is a Grade II listed building. It is situated opposite the Hackney Tearooms. The well dressing festivities in Barlow take place every year on the Wednesday after the Feast of St Lawrence (10th August). Three wells (including the pump) are dressed with flower heads. It is thought that the custom in Barlow either dates from 1840, when the pump was built, or from 1615 as thanksgiving for a continuous water supply throughout a long period of drought.

Cutthorpe - The name means 'Cutt's outlying farm'. Cutthorpe is a small village, which initially made its living from agriculture, but by the early 20th century had four coal mines: one at Four Lane Ends; one near the Methodist chapel; one on Common Lane and one at Ingmanthorpe.

Cutthorpe Hall - The earliest part of the hall dates from the 15th century and was the home of Dr Linacre (mentioned above). The main part was built in 1688, but was extended again in the 19th century. It is said that there is an underground passage from the cellar to a point somewhere outside the grounds. The Heathcote family acquired it from the Foljambes in 1614. Continuing the medical connection with the Royal Family, Gilbert Heathcote was physician to Queen Anne.

Kitchenflat Wood - Until the early 20th century, there were quarries in Kitchenflat Wood. Much of the stone was used for making slop-stones and sinks, hence the name.

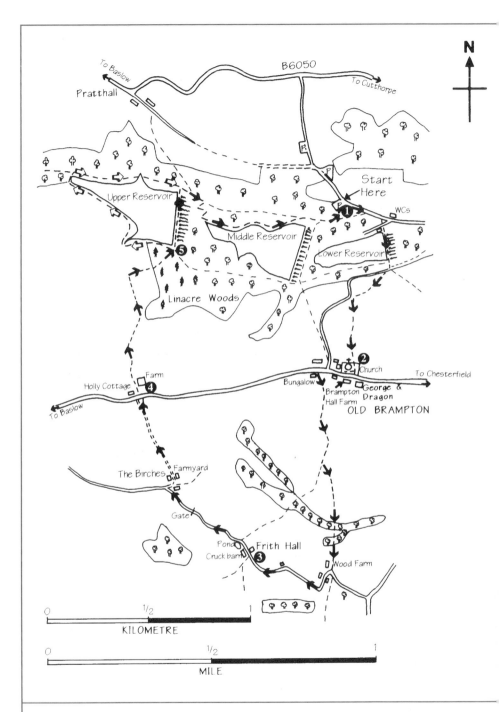

Walk 12 Linacre Woods - Old Brampton - Frith Hall - Linacre Reservoirs

Route: Linacre Woods - Old Brampton - Frith Hall - Linacre Reservoirs

Approximate distance: 4 miles (6.5 km) or 4.8 miles (7.75 km) with optional extension.

Starting point: Linacre Woods car park.

Map reference: SK336727.

Required maps: OS Outdoor Leisure 24 (The White Peak) or Pathfinder 761 (Chesterfield) - both 1:25,000 scale. Alternatively, Landranger 119 (Buxton, Matlock and Dovedale) - 1:50,000 scale.

Terrain: A relatively easy walk, which largely follows easy paths or lanes through woodland, across farmland and which includes the attractive and interesting village of Old Brampton and a cruck barn at Frith Hall. Can be muddy in places.

Refreshments: The George and Dragon, Old Brampton

Approximate time: 2 hours (add 20 minutes for the optional extension).

Public transport: Buses from Chesterfield, Barlow and Holmesfield (limited service).

The Walk

As with Walk 11, this walk starts from the lower of the three visitors' car parks at Linacre Woods ❶. The car parks are approached via a single track road from the B6050 Cutthorpe to Baslow road. Within the woods, there are several picnic sites with tables provided.

With your back to the car park, turn right onto the road and follow it downhill for 200 yards as far as the public conveniences and the Ranger

Old Brampton Church

Station, then take the steps down to the dam wall, passing beside the red roof tiled house. Walk over the dam wall and take the path straight up the bank ahead. Cross over the track that passes left to right and then climb the stile immediately ahead. Head diagonally right and downhill across the field. Follow the path along the bottom side of the field and then take the stile on the left about 20 yards before reaching the bottom right hand corner of the field. Head uphill, to the right hand corner of the field. At the top, cross the stile and follow the path ahead between a hedge and a fence. Head for the church and take the path through the churchyard ❷.

From the churchyard, turn right (i.e.. west) along the road for about 100 yards, then take the path (signposted to "Chander Hill") on the left near a bungalow. Keep to the right hand side of the first three fields. In the fourth field, keep right until halfway along, then strike out half left towards a stone stile halfway along the bottom boundary of the field. In the next field, keep right once more and cross the stile in the bottom right hand corner, into a narrow strip of woodland, over a brook and out the other side. Head uphill across a small field, over another stream, which is culverted, and towards the gap in the trees ahead, then up towards the stone cottage (Wood Farm).

On crossing the stile next to the gate, turn sharp right onto a lane. Follow it past the farm buildings and downhill. The lane then turns sharp right and climbs uphill to Frith Hall, where there is an interesting cruck barn ❸. Pass a small pond and gradually climb uphill towards The Birches, passing through a gate on the way. At The Birches, the track meets another lane. At this point, turn right into the farmyard and then generally bear left between the largest of the farm buildings, emerging onto an open lane, which heads in a straight line towards the Old Brampton road.

At the road, ❹ cross and take the footpath opposite, just to the right of Holly Cottage. Keep to the right of the first two fields, then after 50 yards in the third field take the signposted path diagonally across the field, aiming towards the left hand corner of the nearest woodland. Cross the stile into the next field and keep right. Part way across the following field follow the signpost to the right and keep to the top side of the field as you head towards the wood. In the wood, continue downhill on the broad path to the dam wall, where there are good views up and down the valley as well as a picnic area ❺.

(At this stage, you can opt to take the well-made path around the perimeter of the upper reservoir, which will add a very pleasant 0.8 mile or 1.25 km to the walk.)

Cross the dam wall and take the broad path on the right for about 60 yards, then take the broad path that zigzags downhill. Just before a small concrete footbridge, take the narrower path on the left through the trees and follow this path all the way along the edge of the middle reservoir. Just before the dam wall, the path rejoins the main track. Continue past the dam wall and begin to climb uphill. About 150 yards after the dam wall, take the path on the left that climbs uphill by means of steps and walkways back to the car park.

Linacre Lower Reservoir

Places of Interest

Linacre - The name "Linacre" is derived from the Old English words "Lin" (meaning "flax") and "aecer" (meaning "a plot of arable land"). The flax was probably grown in the valley bottom, where the damp conditions would have been ideal for growing the crop.

Lower Reservoir - The first of the three reservoirs to be built was the lower dam. This was built in 1855 as a response to the need for clean water in Chesterfield, which was growing rapidly. The reservoir holds 31 million gallons when full, covers 8.5 acres and is 31 feet deep.

Old Brampton Church - A church has probably existed on this site from pre Norman times. William II granted a chapelry in 1100 AD. The present church was built in about 1253 and was consecrated on 21 July 1254. The

Old Brampton Church spire

"broach" spire was added in the following century. The church clock was installed in honour of Queen Victoria's Diamond Jubilee in 1897. Somewhat mystifyingly, the clock face contains 63 minutes rather than the usual 60! The church is attractively set within its churchyard, which features two thatched lych gates.

Brampton Old Hall (Hall Farm) - Part of this building dates from the 12th century. Some of the cruck oak beams and timbers are reputed to come from an earlier village church. There is also supposedly a secret passage linking the Hall with the altar in the church.

Frith Hall Cruck Barn - The long stone barn at Frith Hall, although looking more modern from the outside, contains a number of cruck timbers which date from about 1400. The northern end of the barn has a set of cruck timbers exposed. A good place to see the shape of the timbers is from a vantage point just past the pond, which is on the lane beyond the farmyard. The two storey farmhouse was built in 1804.

Upper Reservoir - This was the second of the three reservoirs to be built. It was constructed in 1863-8 and it holds 120 million gallons. It covers 18 acres and is 61 feet deep.

Middle Reservoir - This was built in 1904 and holds 90.5 million gallons. It covers an area of 17 acres and is 42 feet deep.

Cruck barn, Frith Hall

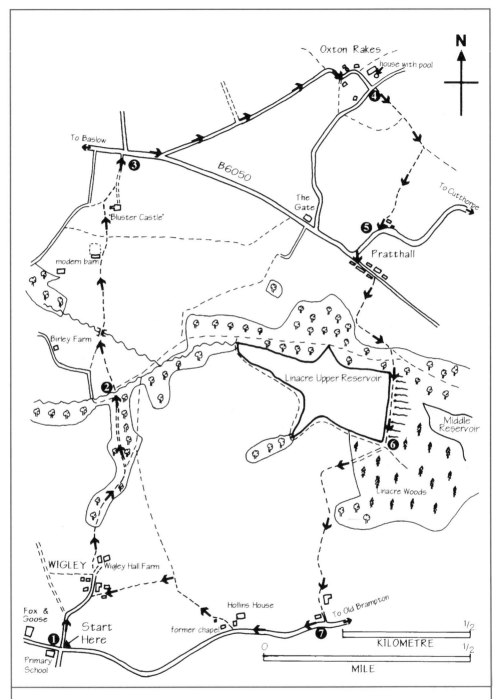

N

To Baslow

B6050

Oxton Rakes

house with pool

The Gate

To Cutthorpe

Pratthall

'Bluster Castle'

modern barn

Birley Farm

Linacre Upper Reservoir

Middle Reservoir

Linacre Woods

WIGLEY

Wigley Hall Farm

Fox & Goose

Start Here

Primary School

Hollins House

former chapel

To Old Brampton

1/2

KILOMETRE

1/2

0

MILE

Walk 13 Wigley, "Bluster Castle", Oxton Rakes, Pratthall, Linacre Reservoirs

Route: Wigley - "Bluster Castle" - Oxton Rakes - Pratthall,
Linacre Reservoirs - Wigley.

Approximate distance: 5 miles (8 km).

Starting point: Wigley Primary School.

Map reference: SK315716.

Required maps: Outdoor Leisure 24 (White Peak) or
Pathfinder 761 (Chesterfield) both 1:25,000 scale. Alternatively,
Landranger 119 (Buxton, Matlock and Dovedale) 1:50,000 scale.

Terrain: Farmland, woodland, reservoir, open views (parts of
walk can be muddy in wet conditions). Several uphill stretches.

Refreshments: The Fox and Goose, Wigley. Also, The Gate,
Pratthall (slight diversion required to reach this pub)

Approximate time: 2 hours 30 minutes

Public transport: Buses from Chesterfield and Baslow.

The Walk

The walk starts outside Wigley Primary School ❶ on the Old Brampton-
Baslow road about one and a half miles west of Old Brampton and near
the Fox & Goose pub. It is possible to park just off the road near the
school.

Start by taking the No Through Road to Wigley opposite the school.
Follow the lane, (ignoring the fork left after 100 yards) past farm buildings
including Wigley Farm. Take the footpath (signposted 'Reservoir') on the
left, past saplings, with a drystone wall to the left. Pass below and to the
left of a stone barn. The path drops downhill for about a quarter of a mile
(it can be very sticky underfoot when wet) and then climbs again through
woodland before reaching a junction. Take the broader path on the left and
follow it downhill until reaching a brook ❷.

View from B6050 near "Bluster Castle" looking towards Chesterfield.

Ford the brook, immediately cross the stile and continue ahead across the field. Reach another stream, which you cross on the small timber footbridge. Climb straight ahead, ignoring sheep tracks that diverge to the right and reach a stile consisting of planks between two trees. Cross into the next field and reach a stile on the right after 100 yards. Then keep left, passing a modern barn (part of Birley Grange farm). At the stone stile continue ahead uphill, aiming just left of the farmhouse on the hilltop (known as "Bluster Castle"), passing through a narrow gap to the right of a metal gate. Then cross the corner of the field to a stile on the right. The path then crosses the next field towards the farm track, which is then followed to the road (B6050), where there are excellent views north towards Holmesfield and also south and east ❸.

Bear right onto the road and after 200 yards take the unsurfaced lane on the left towards Oxton Rakes. This straight lane drops steadily downhill, with excellent views all the way. It can be muddy in places, but after half a mile and close to several cottages, it becomes metalled. Follow the lane past several houses and cottages. Just after a house with a swimming pool in its garden turn left onto an unsurfaced lane, but then immediately take the stile on the right ❹ and continue ahead across the field towards the far left corner. Cross the stream and a stile and continue ahead, keeping to the right boundary. About 10 yards before the end of the field take a right turn at the gate and follow the left side of the next field, reaching a wooden stile in the left corner. Follow the path uphill towards stone cottages on the crest, keeping to the left across several fields ❺.

Turn right onto the road (the B6050 again) and follow it around the left hand bend. After 200 yards, the road bends right. Turn left here and take the lane past several cottages and farm buildings for about 130 yards, before turning right over the stile opposite Pratt Hall. Drop downhill first to one stile then another. Here, turn left and follow the centre of the sloping field towards the woodland. Cross a difficult timber stile and drop down through woodland to the dam wall of Linacre Upper Reservoir. Cross the dam wall with good views up and down the valley. At the far side of the dam there is a picnic area with tables ❻.

Once across the dam wall, ignore the made up path that crosses left to right. Instead, bear half right and uphill along a break in the trees. At the edge of the wood, cross a stile into a field and continue ahead, keeping to the left. At the end of the field cross a stile and turn left. Keep left across two fields before dropping into a slight dip. Cross another stile and head half right uphill, reaching a further stile. Keep left through two more fields, before passing just left of a cottage and reaching the road ❼.

Linacre Upper Reservoir

Bear right and follow the road for almost a quarter of a mile. Just after Hollins House and before a small former Wesleyan Methodist Chapel (dating from 1846), take the signposted path on the right. Pass behind the chapel and into a small field. Head towards a small timber stable, just to the right of which is a stile. In the next field keep to the right and turn right after crossing the stile at the far end. After another 40 yards pass through a narrow gap in the corner of the stone wall and turn left, following the straight (and partially surfaced) track uphill towards the farm on the crest of the hill. Cross the farmyard and reach the lane. Turn left and follow the lane back towards the road and Wigley Primary School.

Wigley Primary School

Places of Interest

Wigley Hall Farm - A three storey stone farmhouse dating from the 17th century and Grade II listed.

Saxon road - The track from Wigley down to the valley bottom and up to Birley Grange is an old route, thought to date back to Anglo-Saxon times.

Birley Farm - The walk passes below this farm. If the weather is exceptionally clear, it may be worth taking a detour, because the view down the valley to Chesterfield is excellent. According to local writer, Roger Redfearn, it is possible to read the clock on Chesterfield church with a good pair of binoculars. It is also possible to spot Lincoln cathedral (50 miles away).

Birley Grange - This farm used to belong to the monks of Louth.

Bluster Castle - Not a castle, but a farmhouse occupying an exposed hilltop position.

Oxton Rakes - The name means ox or oxen paths.

Pratt Hall - The Old Hall, now Pratt Hall Farm, contains cruck timbers. The present hall was built in the 17th century and extended in 1703.

Hollins House - The original hall was demolished in 1826 and was replaced with the present house. There is still an old cruck barn to the left of the house. Hollins House was owned by the Drabble family, who built several Methodist chapels in the area, including one at Pratthall, now demolished.

Methodist Chapel - Now used as a workshop and store, this was built and kept by the Drabble family from 1846 to 1957. It was then bequeathed to the local Methodist circuit, but closed in the early 1960s due to falling attendances. In 1965 it was sold, with a covenant preventing it being used as a house or for the sale of liquor.

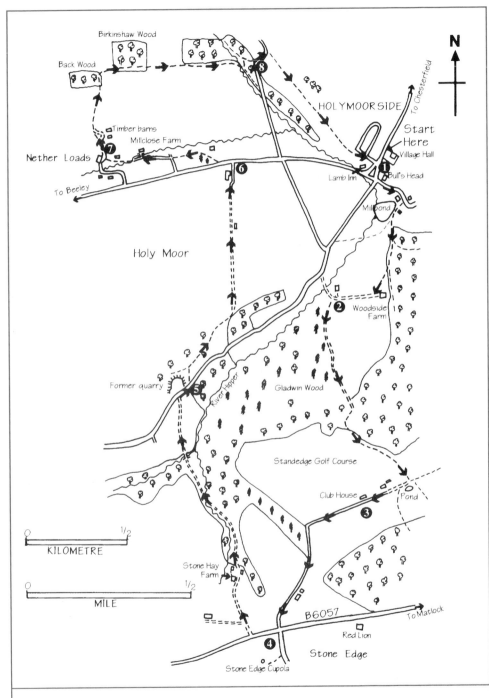

Walk 14 Holymoorside - Stone Edge - Holy Moor - Nether Loads - Holymoorside

Route: Holymoorside - Stone Edge - Holy Moor - Nether Loads - Holymoorside

Approximate distance: 6 miles (9.5 km).

Starting point: Holymoorside Village Hall.

Map reference: SK338694.

Required maps: OS Outdoor Leisure 24 (The White Peak) or Pathfinder 761 (Chesterfield) - both 1:25,000 scale. Alternatively, Landranger 119 (Buxton, Matlock and Dovedale) - 1:50,000 scale.

Terrain: Village, woodland, farmland, golf course, open views, industrial heritage. Mainly on easy tracks, but with some lengthy uphill stretches. Muddy at times.

Refreshments: The Bulls Head and The Lamb Inn, Holymoorside. The Red Lion at Stone Edge.

Approximate time: 2 hours 45 minutes

Public transport: Buses from Chesterfield.

The Walk

The walk starts in the centre of Holymoorside outside the village hall, where there is ample parking on the road ❶.

From the village hall, walk downhill and take the road on the left, next to the Bulls Head pub . Just after the United Reformed Church and before the Church of St Peter, take the path on the right which passes the former millpond (now a fishing lake). Halfway along the side of the pond, take the left hand fork, pass between stone posts and follow a broad track to the left of a hedge towards a wood. Go into the wood and after 100 yards squeeze through a wooden stile and follow the path down a short way out into a field. Continue towards Woodside Farm and turn right onto the

Millpond, Holymoorside

farm track. After 150 yards or so take the path leading uphill to the wood on the left ❷.

Continue uphill for just over a quarter of a mile between stone walls up a rocky lane, with woodland to the right and an open field to the left. The path then bears right in front of a gate. Keep close to the dry stone wall for about 75 yards then follow the path uphill through a tunnel of holly bushes and between saplings and small bushes, as it gradually bears left and levels out.

Pass a golf tee and shortly afterwards emerge onto the Standedge golf course. Heed the warning sign and keep to the left of the fairway until reaching the pond. Here, turn right and follow the stone track past an old farmhouse (keeping an eye out for flying golf balls, but also admiring the extensive view northwards) and then past the club house ❸.

The track, which is now a surfaced lane, is straight for about 400 yards, then turns sharp left and heads down to the Darley Road (B5057), passing a farm and a duckpond. Ahead can be seen a chimney, which is a remnant of the Stone Edge Cupola, and is an ancient monument. If you wish to have a refreshment break, the Red Lion pub is less than quarter of a mile along the road, if you turn left. If you want to have a closer look at the chimney, go up the lane opposite and then take the footpath on the right after 200 yds. This passes within a few yards of the chimney. Return by the same route ❹.

Otherwise, at the road turn right for 100 yards, then right again down a farm track. Ignore the track which forks to the left almost immediately and continue downhill, passing Stone Hay Farm. Go through the farmyard, and take the grassy lane which leaves from the right hand corner of the farmyard. The track descends between dry stone walls into woodland, eventually crossing a stream. Continue on the obvious track, dropping down and reaching the River Hipper after another 250 yards. Cross over the river on the footbridge and climb uphill for about 200 yards. At the road (Harewood Road) turn right for 50 yards, then take the bridleway on the left ❺.

Climb for 50 yards, then bear right on the same track through trees and saplings. As you climb, the trees gradually give way to bracken and gorse and there are excellent views towards Chesterfield and the woods on the opposite side of the valley. The path climbs gently and then levels out before turning sharp left at a drystone wall. The path is now dead straight and between stone walls across Holy Moor (these days mainly farmland), with a gentle downhill gradient.

At the road ❻ turn left (or right if you want to take a shortcut back into Holymoorside). After 50 yds, take the path on the right (signposted Upper Loads) The path follows the right hand side of a small wood for a short distance to a gap in a dry stone wall, cuts across a small field, through another gap and then between gorse bushes.

At the lane, bear right and continue straight ahead. As you pass the small stone cottage (Millclose Farm), the lane becomes grassy before crossing a stream into the field ahead. Proceed towards the stone barn at the end of the field, then through the wooden gate, along to a stone stile and turn right onto the lane at the farmhouse (Nether Loads) ❼.

Follow the lane uphill. Where the lane kinks right then left, continue ahead keeping close to the stone wall on the left. Reach a wall with a metal gate, climb the stile to the left of the gate and enter a large field, sometimes with

Church of St. Peter, Holymoorside

plenty of rabbits in it! Strike out half right, aiming for the right hand corner of the wood in front of you.

At the corner of the wood, the path follows the inside edge of the wood to the left of the gate and the fence. (NB It can be very boggy here at times.) Climb slightly for 50 yards and then bear right into a field, following the right hand side of the field alongside a holly hedge. Stay on the track through the top of Burkinshaw Wood, then reach a metal gate and squeeze through the stile just to the left. Once through, keep to the left of the next field, ignoring the track that goes diagonally to the right. At the left corner of the field, the path dips between the holly bushes, and a stile takes you into the next field. Keep left as you descend and cross the next stile. Continue ahead and cross the footbridge over a brook, then immediately bear left and up to a stile. Over the stile turn acute right uphill, reaching a further stile at a road ❽.

Turn left up the road for 50 yards or so, then sharp right over a stone stile into a field. Keep to the right of the first field and then the centre of the next three, as you follow a ridge and gradually drop down into Holymoorside. Emerge onto a housing estate road. Follow this downhill into the centre of the village, with the village hall directly ahead.

Places of Interest

Holymoorside - As a village, Holymoorside has existed for only 200 years, and was previously only a small hamlet consisting of a few farms. The village developed as a mill town in the early 19th century, with new houses being built to house recruited labour. Until 1831, the village was within the Parish of Brampton. The name 'Holymoorside' is not derived from any religious connection, but is thought to be Norse in origin, i.e. 'hóh léah' (hill clearing) plus 'mór' (hill spur). There is a hill spur which juts out near the present day Sycamore Farm.

St Peter's Church - Was built in 1841 as a schoolroom and as a place of worship. This small stone building is a contrast to the grand parish churches in nearby and longer established villages.

Millpond - The millpond was built to power the Holymoor mills (of which more in the next chapter), but is now used mainly by ducks and fishermen.

Cathole Mill - This was sited in the hollow near ❷ where there are now some houses and a copse. The mill was built in the 1820s and was owned by the Cundey family, who manufactured bobbins. It had an 18ft water wheel, which was fed from a mill pond. In 1832, the mill was sold to George Bingham, but was subsequently sold in 1851 to Simeon Manlove, the owner of Holymoor Mills. He converted it into a dye works, and it stayed in this use until it was closed in 1902.

Stone Edge Cupola and Lead Smelting - This gets a mention in the Guinness Book of Records as the oldest freestanding chimney in the country. It was built in the 1770s and is listed as an ancient monument. To visit the actual site, you should first apply at Spitewinter Farm (nearby) to the owners, but there is a footpath that passes close to the chimney (see walk description).

The chimney was used for lead smelting, using the cupola process, which was invented in 1735. The lead ore was put in above a layer of wood. The flames from the fire passed over the ore and were reflected by the top of the kiln, magnifying the intensity of the blaze. The fire was fanned by water powered bellows, which were driven by water from a small reservoir nearby.

The cupola method replaced the earlier boles and ore hearths, which had been prevalent for centuries. Boles were crude hearths 3 to 5 feet deep, which were always located on windy hilltops, to fan the blaze and disperse poisonous fumes. Alternate layers of ore and firewood were placed in the hole and ignited. The melted lead would run through prepared cavities where it was collected. This method was used by the Romans and continued until superseded by furnaces and cupolas. Although cupolas were more efficient, not all the lead was extracted at first, so the remaining ore would be taken away for re-smelting elsewhere. The second smelting produced a harder lead, which was ideal for making lead shot and red lead.

Quarrying - There were numerous quarries in the area. The local stone is sandstone, although there is also brick shale, clay and gannister. Gannister is a fine grained stone used to make furnace linings and other refractories.

Stone Edge Cupola.

Nether Loads - In the 18th and 19th centuries there were several small millponds in this area and a small mill. The name 'Millclose Farm' bears witness to this. The mill was a small smelting works, which manufactured red lead. This would have been a dirty and polluting operation. In about 1800, the mill ceased being used for lead smelting and became a corn mill. Given the toxic nature of red lead, the flour must surely have been tainted! There is also evidence that there was a brick kiln in the field between Millclose Farm and Nether Loads Farm, although there are no physical remains to be seen. This kiln apparently manufactured high quality bricks.

The Lamb Inn - This has been a public house since 1850, although the building is much older. The date stone on the building dates it to 1760.

Walk 15 Holymoorside - Harper Hill - Great Pond of Stubbing - Stone Edge - Gladwin Wood - Holymoorside.

Route: Holymoorside - Harper Hill - Great Pond of Stubbing - Stone Edge - Gladwin Wood - Holymoorside.

Approximate distance: 6.5 miles (10 km)

Starting point: Holymoorside Village Hall.

Map reference: SK338694

Required maps: Pathfinder 761 (Chesterfield) - 1:25,000 scale. Alternatively, Landranger 119 (Buxton, Matlock and Dovedale) - 1:50,000 scale.

Terrain: Village, farmland, woodland, lake, golf course, open views. Some lengthy uphill stretches.

Refreshments: The Bulls Head and The Lamb Inn, Holymoorside. The Red Lion, Stone Edge.

Approximate time: 3 hours

Public transport: Buses from Chesterfield.

The Walk

The walk starts in the centre of Holymoorside outside the village hall ❶, where there is ample parking.

From the village hall, turn left at the Bulls Head pub and follow the road past the United Reformed Church. In front of a large stone house (Rose Cottage), turn left onto and grassy lane and pass behind the gardens of several houses. (The houses are on the site of the Holymoor Mills, which were in operation between the late 18th century and 1902.) Emerge from the lane and continue ahead across two fields and cross a concreted farm track into another field. Cross the stile at the furthest end of the field onto a lane ❷.

Harper Hill House

Go along the farm track opposite and, after passing the farmhouse and some outbuildings, cross the stile on the left (next to a gate). Cross the field on a track initially and head for the stile in the far left hand corner. Keep to the left through three more fields. In the fourth field, cross a stile to the left after 50 yds. Head downhill, bearing just right of the farm and barn to a wooden stile on the left about 10 yds before the end of the field. Follow the path between wire fences down to a wooden footbridge. Continue uphill until you reach the main road (A632) ❸.

Turn left and follow the road for about 200 yds, then cross over and take the overgrown lane on the right (signposted). After a short distance, emerge onto a wider lane and continue straight ahead towards Broadgorse Farm, going through a wooden gate. About 50 yds before the farm itself cross the stone stile on the right and keep to the left of the field down to the fence and stile. Turn left for 50 yds, then cross the stream and climb uphill, ignoring the stile on the left at the bottom of the field. Near the top, cross a stile and follow the right hand side of the next field up to the lane at Harper Hill.

Turn right and continue for about 200 yds, turning left at the signpost ("Watson Lane"). Follow the track between the houses, down the right hand side of the field. The path goes right for 10 yds, then turns left and follows an attractive, broad track along the valley top through mature oak woodland. Continue on this track for about half a mile or so and emerge from the wood, with a view down to the Great Pond of Stubbing on the right. Pass through the gate and onto the lane. Continue downhill a few yards and then turn right onto the dam wall ❹.

On the far side, take the stone farm track almost opposite and follow it up past Stubbing Court Home Farm. Keep to the stone wall on the right, which marks the boundary of the parkland of Stubbing Court. Follow the wall for about 250 yds after the farm, curving first right, then left and right again. Then bear half left across the field (note the small yellow waymark on a white post) towards a stile beneath a pair of beech trees and then along the left hand side of the next field. In the far left hand corner go through a gap and bear diagonally right across the following field towards woodland Continue with the wood to your left for about 300 yds before reaching a stile and gate.

Go directly across the large field towards a gate and a signpost. Keep to the right of the next field, going through the gap at the end. Continue ahead through a muddy area to the very end of the field, passing a stone cottage. In the right hand corner of the field, cross the stile into a small field with a very high Leylandii hedge on your right. At the farm lane, turn left and follow it past some timber poultry sheds, and turn sharp right near some propane tanks. Almost immediately and just before the next set of poultry sheds, turn left onto the path, crossing a stile near the stream ❺.

Climb uphill towards Stone Edge Farm. Bear just to the left of the farm buildings across a concreted area to a stile and gate. Then cross diagonally uphill for 50 yds to a stile, emerging onto a farm lane. Turn left along the lane and continue for 100 yds, then turn right at a stile and gate. Climb uphill, reaching a metal bar stile. Pass a belt of woodland and a timber summer house and reach the main road (A632). (Here you can opt to cross over and follow the road opposite for about quarter of a mile to The Red Lion, if you want some refreshment.)

Turn right along the A632 for about 80 yds and then turn left and go through the gap behind the bus stop sign. Take the right hand of the two paths through Stone Edge Plantation. Continue ahead for about 250 yds ignoring paths that fork or cross. You will reach a major fork; take the right hand fork. Shortly afterwards, a major path crosses right to left. Ignore this and continue ahead. At the far side of the wood, cross the broken down stone wall onto Standedge Golf course, observing the warning notices, and head straight ahead downhill towards the old stone house. Bear right along the lane in front of the house, and continue for about 150 yds before reaching a small pond. Here there are excellent views north towards Chesterfield and Sheffield. At the pond, turn left and keep to the right of the fairway until reaching a white sign ❻.

Follow the path into the woodland on the right hand side. At first the path is narrow and winds between saplings, holly bushes, etc., but gradually bears right and drops downhill, before reaching an unsurfaced lane. Bear left onto this lane and follow it downhill for just over quarter of a mile, with open fields on the right and woodland to the left.

At the bottom of the lane, enter a field and turn right onto a farm track. About 50 yds before reaching Woodside Farm, bear left across the field towards woodland and a stile. Stay close to the wall on the left within the wood and follow the path out into a field. Pass the old millpond, go along a driveway and emerge onto a road. Turn left and follow the road back into Holymoorside, past the Bulls Head and back to your starting point.

Places of Interest

Holymoor Mills - The Holymoor Mills were on the site now occupied by the houses on Riverside Crescent. The stone house at the corner of Riverside Crescent, which survives, was the mill office. The mills were powered by water from the dam to the rear of the Congregational Chapel and had been built in the late 18th century. In the late 1830s, Simeon Manlove purchased the mills and set about transforming the business. He specialised in high quality sewing cottons, selling to the household and specialist markets, exporting a good deal of the production. The main reason for the siting of the mills in a relatively cut off location was the presence of water to power the mills.

Former Mill Offices

Soon the operation outgrew the population, so Manlove built houses to accommodate more workers, many of whom were specialised silk winders from Manchester and Macclesfield. In 1861, 130 people were employed, which grew to 209 by 1871. In 1872, three families from Cornwall were induced to move to the village.

As noted in the previous chapter, Manlove also acquired the nearby Cathole Mill and used this for dying his cotton products. The presence of the mills virtually accounted for the growth of Holymoorside from a cluster of a few farms to a sizeable village. When the Manlove family sold out to the English Sewing Cotton Company in 1897, which was an agglomeration of the largest cotton thread manufacturers, little did they realise that by 1902 the mills would be closed as part of a 'rationalisation'

Stubbing Court

exercise. This had a catastrophic effect on the village. Some workers had to move to Skipton or Scotland to find work.

Harper Hill House - This unusual house was built in about 1842 by the Hunloke family. The first tenant was the vicar of Wingerworth, Rev. Samuel Revel.

Great Pond of Stubbing - The pond was built by the Hunlokes in the 18th century as an ornamental fishing lake. Surprisingly, Stubbing Court was not owned by the Hunlokes, although the house derives the most benefit from the lake by virtue of its close proximity.

Stubbing Court - The house was once owned by Henry Gladwin (b. 1729, d. 1791), whose main claim to fame was his army career in the American Colonies, particularly his defence of Fort Detroit against Pontiac. Gladwin had the present façade constructed, which overlooks the Great Pond. Another famous resident was the daughter of Harold Soames, who later married the founder of the scouting movement and became Lady Baden-Powell. The house is not open to the public.

Stone Edge Plantation - A large hilltop plantation that was planted by Sir Henry Hunloke IV. Previously the site had been quarried, and the remains can still be seen.

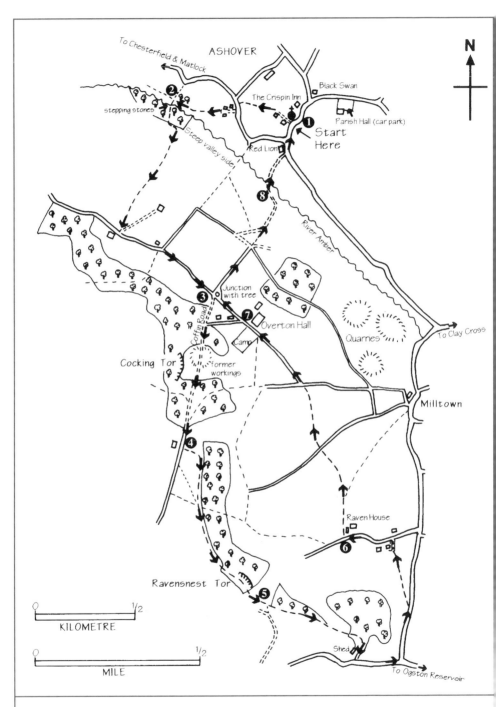

Walk 16 Ashover - Ravensnest Wood and Tor - Overton - Ashover

Route: Ashover - Ravensnest Wood and Tor - Overton -
Ashover

Approximate distance: 5.25 miles (8 km)

Starting point: All Saints Church, Ashover.

Map reference: SK348632.

Required maps: Pathfinder 761 (Chesterfield) 1:25,000 scale.
Alternatively, Landranger 119 (Buxton, Matlock & Dovedale)
1:50,000 scale.

Terrain: Initially a good deal of ascent, which is rewarded with
stunning views. Woodland, packhorse road, farmland, remnants
of old industry.

Refreshments: The Red Lion, The Crispin Inn and The Black
Swan, Ashover

Approximate time: 3 hours

Public transport: Buses from Chesterfield and Clay Cross.

The Walk

The walk starts from the centre of Ashover on Church Street outside All
Saints parish church ❶. It is sometimes possible to park on the street, but if
it is busy, there is a free car park signposted.

Take the driveway to the left of the church, past Chantry House and
Delphi Cottage and bear half left between a fence and a Leylandii hedge.
Keep to the left as you cross the school playing fields. At the far corner,
take the path between a wall and a beech hedge to the road. Turn left for
40 yds then right at the signpost, going up a track to some cottages, across
a concrete apron and to an iron gate. Then cross the field heading down to
the lower section, and enter woodland at the far end. Cross a stile, a stone

footbridge and a timber footbridge with a stile. Cross a small grassy area to another stile over a barbed wire fence into a large open area ❷.

Turn 90° left and follow the fence to the river. Cross the river by the stepping stones and climb steeply up through the wood, following the path with the timber steps (NB this path is very slippery when wet). At the top, emerge into a field through a wall made of vertical flagstones. Turn left and follow the flagstones to the stile. Then bear diagonally right and proceed up the field to a point just to the left of a clump of bushes. The farmer has removed the stile, but the wall is low at this point. Cross over and follow the right hand side of the field to a gate. Then follow the left hand side of the next field and turn left at the lane. Follow the lane for almost half a mile, before reaching a crossroads of lanes and paths with a large central tree ❸.

Bear right onto the track, which is a former packhorse road and is also known as the "Coffin Road". This is surfaced in stone flags. The flags peter out and the path broadens out as it climbs through woodland with rhododendron bushes, and passes a stone drinking trough. Eventually reach an open area, with the remains of old lead workings. There is a stone chimney visible down on the left. Follow the same line through to the other side and enter woodland once again. The track then becomes surfaced and after 100 yds or so there is a modern farm building on the right. Opposite this, on the left, is a stone stile ❹. Descend through bracken (dense in the summer, but less evident at other times of the year) towards the wood and bear right.

Follow the path along the upper boundary of the wood for almost half a mile, ignoring various stiles on the left. The woodland falls away steeply and affords glimpses of precipitous drops. Eventually, reach a stile ahead of you in a stone wall and pass into the wood. The path follows the top of the wood closely for about 200 yds, before emerging ahead through a stile onto open heathland (NB the stile is slightly hidden by a tree). Suddenly there are dramatic views of Ogston, Tupton, Milltown and beyond. This is a good spot for a break on a fine day ❺.

Follow the top of the escarpment and drop down towards the next wood. Continue through the wood as the path begins to curve to the right and reach an old store shed. Pass through a small yard to reach the road and turn left. After 250 yds take the left turning. After another 250 yds, bear half left at a gate and across a field (which may have a barbed wire fence across it with a small wooden stile) to a ditch with a stone footbridge and stile. Then, crossing a second field, keep left and climb over a stone stile in the very corner. Cross the small field towards the nearest house, keeping left, then follow the path to the side of the driveway to the road. Turn left and follow the private road past Raven House and its outbuildings, taking the path on the right immediately after the last farm drive ❻.

Cross towards the centre of the far field boundary and bear left in the next field towards a hedge and continue to the next stile, which has metal posts. Keep to the left and reach a lane. Cross over and take the path opposite, keeping left as the path climbs slightly uphill. At the top of the field, cross the stone stile into a small field and proceed up to a junction between two lanes. Take the lane straight ahead and after quarter of a mile pass Overton Park Camp and Overton Hall ❼.

Outside the entrance to the hall, take the right fork and continue along the lane until reaching the junction with the large central tree. Turn right and continue until the next crossroads is reached. Take the path directly ahead, between the gap in the upright flagstones and proceed downhill to the bottom of the field. Cross the stile, continue down and join the lane, following this downhill until it levels out and swings left ❽, then bear right and uphill into Ashover. At the road turn left, pass The Red Lion Inn and then turn right onto Church Street to return to your starting point.

View of Ashover from Overton

Places of Interest

Ashover - A settlement has existed here since at least Saxon times, when the village was known as 'Essovere', which literally means 'ash tree slope'

All Saints Church - The present church is not the first on this site, but was built between 1350 and 1419. Thomas Babington built the particularly graceful spire. Babington is also credited with building the original part of The Crispin Inn adjacent, which has its own history that is summarised on a large signboard on the front of the pub.

Ashover Light Railway - The railway was built by the Clay Cross Company between 1922 and 1925 to transport limestone and fluorspar to their works at Clay Cross. For a time, there was a passenger service, but that soon fell victim to competition from buses and regular services ceased in 1931. The railway closed to all traffic in 1950. The terminus and sidings were located in the broad, flat grassy area near ❷ on the map. The walk briefly follows the former line of the railway near ❸ on the map. The railway can never be reopened, as part of the route now lies flooded beneath Ogston Reservoir.

The Coffin Road - This old way is known as 'The Coffin Road' because corpses were brought from outlying villages such as Dethick and Lea, which had no burial grounds. The route is also a former packhorse road and is still paved in places with small flagstones.

Gregory Mine - This was located near ❼ on the map and was one of the most significant lead mines in the area. The land has recently been reclaimed, so there is relatively little to see. Mining started in the mid 17th century. By 1767, output had exceeded 1,000 tons per annum and profits were in excess of £15,000. However, the business soon peaked and by 1803 the mine was closed. This was partly due to the cost of pumping water to prevent flooding and also because the best vein had been worked out.

Overton - 'Overton' means 'upper farm', being derived from 'uferra tun'.

Overton Hall - The hall was originally owned by the Overton family, but it passed to the Hunts in the 14th century. Subsequently, the estate was divided and the house came into the ownership of the Hodgkinsons in 1599. There are a couple of date stones in the boundary walls which refer

William and Elizabeth Hodkinson and are dated 1699 and 1702 respectively.

The Banks family eventually inherited the estate, the most famous family member being Sir Joseph Banks, who was a celebrated naturalist. He sailed with Captain Cook and became President of the Royal Society.

In February 1887, whilst workmen were excavating in the grounds, several skeletons were discovered in a mass grave. The burials looked hurried and, although there has been some speculation that these were lead mine workers from Roman times, they could well have been plague victims. The bodies were re-interred at Ashover churchyard.

In the early 20th century, the estate was acquired by the Clay Cross Company, principally so that the fluorspar and limestone deposits in the ,000 acres of the estate could be exploited. The Hall was until quite recently used as a local authority old peoples' home, but at the time of writing appears to be in private ownership.

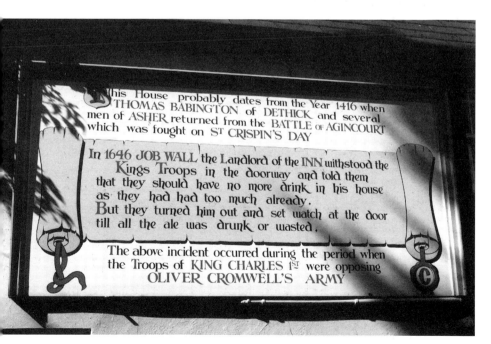

The Crispin Inn, Ashover.

Walk 17 Eastwood Hall - Handley - Ogston Reservoir - Milltown - Overton - Ashover

Route: Ashover - Eastwood Hall - Handley - Ogston Reservoir - Milltown - Overton - Ashover

Approximate distance: 5.6 miles (9 km)

Starting point: All Saints Church, Ashover.

Map reference: SK348632.

Required maps: Pathfinder 761 (Chesterfield) 1:25,000 scale or Landranger 119 Buxton, Matlock & Dovedale 1:50,000 scale.

Terrain: Farmland, woodland, reservoir. Fairly easy going on paths with short steep sections. Can be muddy in places.

Refreshments: Red Lion, The Crispin Inn and The Black Swan, Ashover; New Napoleon, Woolley Moor/Ogston; Miners Arms, Milltown.

Approximate time: 2 hours 45 minutes.

Public transport: Buses from Chesterfield, Matlock and Clay Cross

The Walk

As with Walk 16, this walk starts in the centre of Ashover, ❶ opposite All Saints Church and The Crispin Inn. It is sometimes possible to park on the street, but there is a free car park 100 yds away near the Parish Hall.

Start by taking the track to the left of the old schoolhouse directly opposite The Crispin Inn. Follow along, passing the sports ground. Pass through a stile and then about 200 yds afterwards turn left, cross two fields and reach the road. Turn right along the road for 250 yds, then take the path on the left immediately before the farm and to the left of the farm driveway. Keep to the right, crossing three fields in the direction of Eastwood Hall (an ivy clad ruin, with the present day farmhouse attached to it), and cross a stile on the right. Pass the front of the Hall and farmhouse and go through the farmyard ❷.

Turn left up the lane, towards the trees and climb as far as the left hand hairpin bend. Just after the hairpin bend bear right into the trees between stone posts. Take the right hand fork through the trees and brambles, emerging on the right hand side of a garden. Follow the path between the wall and hedge (it may be overgrown in summer) to a stile.

Cross over the road and take the path opposite through the double gates. Head straight downhill (NB the field boundaries shown on the OS map have been removed), past the electricity pole to a band of trees. Go down through the wood and cross the field to the stile in the corner. Then head half right uphill aiming just to the right of the farm ahead. At the farm, turn left onto the farm lane passing a small duck pond. At the road turn right for 50 yds, then bear left down a lane, reaching Woodhouse Grange ❸.

Go around the rear of the outbuildings, towards the stile hidden in the bushes. Keep to the left across two fields, and squeeze thorough the stone stile. Head half right and uphill to the next stile, then head towards the stile in the hedge ahead. For the entire length of the next field, keep left and then head diagonally to the top corner of the following field. At the top, go through the gap to reach the lane, then turn left to reach the crossroads at Handley ❹.

Turn right and follow the road past the former Methodist chapel (a date stone on the building says "Methodist New Connexions 1874") and bear left near the bend in the road, taking the left hand of the two paths, which will take you down to the bottom left corner of the field.

All Saints Church, Ashover

Cross the corner of the next field to the road and proceed along the track opposite, crossing through the hedge ahead. Head across the first field, then bear diagonally right across the next two fields. Turn left down the road to the reservoir. Here you can eat or drink at the New Napoleon, which has a large beer garden with play area and views over the reservoir. Alternatively, a few hundred yards to the left there is a picnic site ❺.

Ashover, with flagstone wall in foreground

Turn right and follow the lakeside road for nearly quarter of a mile, then turn right onto the footpath just after Smithy Cottage. Follow the path across two fields and into a wood. Keep to the left whilst crossing three more fields. Halfway along the third field, go through the gate and follow the track, until it leads out onto a lane at a crossroads. Turn sharp left for 30 yds, then look for the stile on the right, which may be obscured by bracken. Once through the stile, continue straight ahead across three fields, reaching a driveway. Bear right and follow the driveway down to a road. Turn right and follow the road for about quarter of a mile until reaching the Miners Arms pub ❻.

Take the path that passes just left of the pub and heads into the trees. After less than 100 yds, bear left along a path that climbs to the left of a quarry and leads out into fields. Keep to the right of the fields until reaching a road at a 90° bend. At this point, turn right up the narrow lane and stay on this lane as it climbs uphill and eventually levels out somewhat. The lane passes to the left of the Milltown Quarry, although this is only really visible at one point. Eventually the lane passes through woodland and behind Overton Hall (which is not visible). Look out for the stone in the wall on the left that bears the inscription "WEH 1699" ❼.

Shortly after passing the inscription, you will reach a crossroads. Continue ahead for 80 yds on the paved path, with a wall of standing flagstones to the right. Then bear right and downhill on the paved lane. Eventually the lane levels out, turns left for a few yards (following the course of the former Ashover Light Railway - long since dismantled), then bears right and uphill into Ashover village. Turn left, pass the Red Lion and turn right onto Church Street, returning to your starting point.

Places of Interest

The remains of Eastwood Hall behind the farmhouse

Old Schoolhouse - This was built in 1877 as a girls' school, despite the motto, which reads: "Train up the child in the way *he* should go and when *he* is old *he* will not depart from it." (My italics.) The building is now used as parish rooms.

Eastwood Hall - Eastwood Hall has a long history and has been a ruin since the time of the English Civil War in 1646, when the Roundheads ransacked it in reprisal for Royalist support. For 340 years it was in the ownership of the Reresby family, but was sold in 1623 to pay off Sir Thomas Reresby's considerable debts. It was purchased by Revd.

Emmanuel Bourne, only to see it destroyed a few years later. The ruins are now unsafe, although the present day farmhouse directly abuts them!

Ogston Reservoir - The valley was flooded in 1958, as water was required for the NCB carbonisation plant at Wingerworth (the largest in Europe at the time). The reservoir covers over 200 acres and has a volume of 1,300 million gallons.

The Miners Arms, Milltown

New Napoleon - This public house was moved up the valley side when Ogston reservoir was built. For 300 years the original building was owned by the Fox family. An ancestor, Mark 'Napoleon' Eliot, was in France at the time of the French Revolution. He made a sign which said "Napoleon's Home" and sent it home to Derbyshire. The inn used this name for many years, but later became known as the Traveller's Rest. It was only when the present building was moved that the Napoleon name was restored.

The Miners' Arms - This pub takes its name from the lead miners who worked the nearby lead mines in the 19th century and the building dates from about 1850.

Quarries - The area around Ashover has a complex geology. Not only is there limestone, but also millstone grit and volcanic tuff (toadstone). The area is and has been rich in mineral deposits, lead mining and fluorspar extraction having been major industries in the past. There are numerous 'rakes', which are long straight veins of ore between vertical walls of surrounding rock. Today, quarrying continues around Ashover for both gritstone and limestone.

William and Elizabeth Hodgkinson of Overton Hall - There are two date stones in the boundary wall of Overton Hall. One reads WEH 1699, the other HW+E 1702. Both refer to William and Elizabeth Hodgkinson, who owned the Hall at the time.

Date stone in boundary wall of Overton Hall

Subsequently, the Hall passed to the Banks family, the most famous member of which was Sir Joseph Banks, who sailed with Captain Cook in 1786. He was also President of the Royal Society and a well-respected naturalist

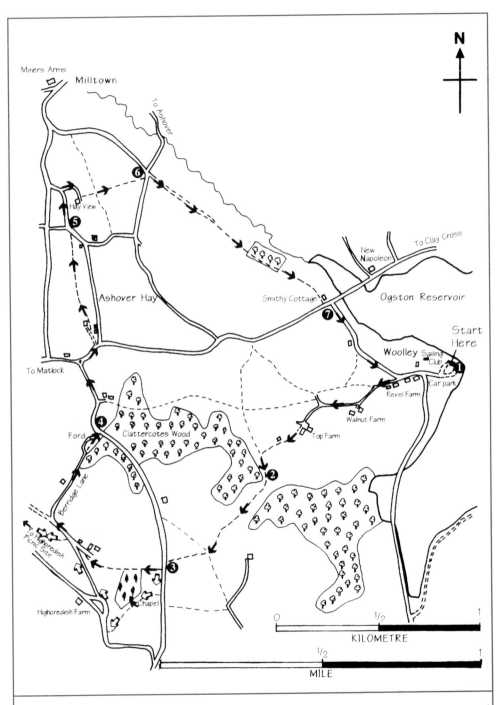

Walk 18 Ogston Reservoir - Woolley - Highoredish - Ashover Hay - Milltown - Ogston Reservoir

Route: Ogston Reservoir - Woolley - Highoredish - Ashover
Hay - Milltown - Ogston Reservoir

Approximate distance: 7.5 km (4.75 miles)

Starting point: Ogston Reservoir Car Park.

Map reference: SK373605

Required maps: Pathfinder 761 (Chesterfield) and 794 (Crich),
both 1:25,000 scale. Alternatively, Landranger 119 (Buxton,
Matlock & Dovedale) 1:50,000 scale.

Terrain: Reservoir, farmland, woodland, open views, one
prolonged steep uphill section.

Refreshments: Miners Arms, Milltown; New Napoleon,
Woolley Moor/Ogston

Approximate time: 2 hours 20 minutes.

Public transport: Buses to Woolley Moor from Matlock, Clay
Cross and Chesterfield.

The Walk

The walk starts from the Ogston Reservoir car park on the west side of the
reservoir ❶. The car park is owned by Severn Trent Water and is open daily
between 6.30 am and 9.30 pm. It's a good spot for a picnic with a good
view of the reservoir and the boats that sail there.

From the car park, head back to the road and follow it uphill for about 130
yds until it bends sharp right. Take the narrow lane uphill, past Revel
Farm and another house. Ignore the path on the right and continue past
Walnut Farm until the end of the lane at Top Farm. Continue ahead
through the muddy farmyard and through a gate into fields. Walk straight
ahead downhill and go through the right hand of the two gates near a
stone outbuilding. Keep to the left side of the next field and turn sharp left

at the end. Keep to the upper boundary of the following field and drop down to the timber stile at the end ❷.

Cross the stream and follow the path uphill to the top of the field, then go through a wide gap in the stone wall and again keep to the left. At the end, cross the stone stile and footbridge and then turn right and follow the path to the road. Turn left for 40 yds, then take the signposted path uphill to the right of the wood ❸.

View of Ashover from Highoredish picnic site

Here you can alternatively stay on the road a little longer and then take the next path on the right, which takes you to the ruins of Trinity Chapel on the left hand side of the wood. Follow the red and black waymark signs that have been provided by Derbyshire County Council. Climb uphill for about a 300 yds after Trinity Chapel and reach a lane. Turn right and follow for about quarter of a mile to rejoin the route of this walk.

Climb steeply and at the top, cross the stone stile and pause for a good view of Ogston Reservoir and Ashover (and to get your breath!). Then continue ahead to Nether Highoredish Farm, joining the farm lane and a short distance later bearing right at the junction. If you wish to stop at Highoredish picnic site, take the path on the left (red waymark signs) and follow a short distance to the picnic site, which has breathtaking views of the Amber valley. Otherwise, continue on the lane, turning sharp right and dropping downhill quite steeply after 100 yds. Stay on the lane until reaching the waymarked footpath on the right about 20 yds before the 'Ford' road sign. Drop downhill across a small field for 100 yds before rejoining the lane near the ford. Continue uphill and then turn left at the T-junction onto a broader lane ❹.

Continue for about quarter of a mile, until reaching the 'Give Way' sign. Bear right and climb uphill on the B road for about 150 yds until reaching the crest of the hill. Turn left up the gravel driveway (as opposed to the nearby lane signposted for Ashover Hay) and climb towards the house on the hilltop. Just before reaching the house itself, go through the gap to the right of the driveway and continue ahead below the house, through a gate and into a field. At the end, cross slightly left through the broad gap in the walls and follow the path along the top of the ridge. Keep just to the left of the stone walls, dropping gradually as you go, with excellent views on either side, eventually reaching a lane ❺.

Bear left and continue in a generally northerly direction towards Milltown. Pass several houses and after about 250 yds turn right at a wooden signpost onto a smaller lane, which climbs and curves to the right. (At this point, you can continue straight ahead into Milltown and to the Miners Arms Inn and then return by the same route.) Just before "Hay View", take the path on the left over the stile and follow the path ahead across three fields until reaching another lane ❻.

At the lane, turn left for 30 yds, then right at the wooden signpost onto an unmade and straight lane. Follow this for about 300 yds, past the metal gate into a field and then slightly downhill until reaching a point where there is a metal gate on the left and a gap on the right. The path goes left through the gate and follows the right side of the next three fields with a view left down to the valley bottom. Then go through a small and steeply sloping wood, before emerging into fields once more. Follow the path to the road crossing two fields on the way.

At the road ❼, cross almost straight over and take the road opposite towards Woolley (You can turn left here, if you wish to divert to the New Napoleon Inn). Stay on the road for just over quarter of a mile , passing the former Methodist Chapel along the way and return to your starting point at the reservoir car park.

Ogston Reservoir

Places of Interest

Woolley - 'Woolley' means 'wolves clearing'.

Ogston Reservoir - The valley was flooded in 1958, as water was required for the NCB carbonisation plant at Wingerworth (the largest in Europe at the time). The reservoir covers over 200 acres and has a volume of 1,300 million gallons. There are two public car parks and the reservoir is a popular destination for sailors, bird watchers and anglers.

Trinity Chapel - You can take a slight diversion from the route of the walk to the remains of Trinity Chapel, some of which is a 16th century building. It was abandoned in 1856, and left to decay, following the construction of a church in nearby Brackenfield. It is thought that this building is on the site of an even earlier chapel.

Highoredish Picnic Site - 'Oredish' is a local family name. The picnic site was opened in 1984 by Derbyshire County Council and is on the site of an old gritstone quarry. There are picnic tables and a viewfinder (vandalised in 1997!).

Clattercotes - 'Clattercotes' means 'cottages near pile of stones' (from 'clater' and 'cot').

View of Ogston Reservoir from Highoredish

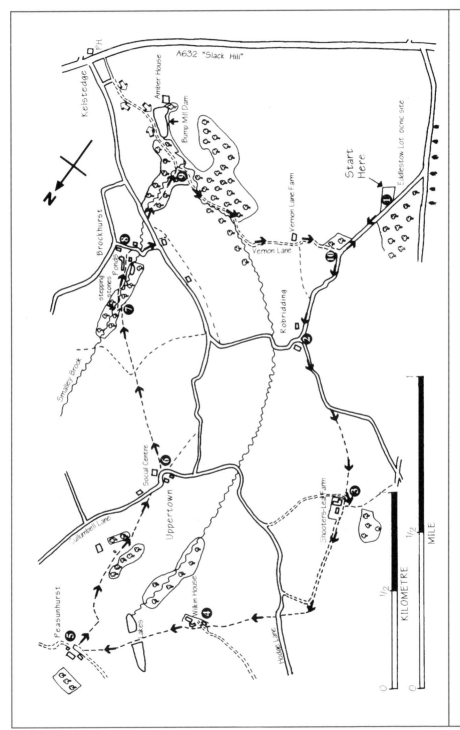

Walk 19 Eddlestow Lot picnic site - Hodge Lane - Peasunhurst - Uppertown - Smalley Brook - Vernon Lane (packhorse road) Eddlestow Lot.

Route: Eddlestow Lot picnic site - Hodge Lane - Peasunhurst - Uppertown - Smalley Brook - Vernon Lane (packhorse road) Eddlestow Lot.

Approximate distance: 5 miles (8 km) or 6 miles (9.5 km) with optional extension.

Starting point: Eddlestow Lot picnic site, near Slack Hill, Kelstedge.

Map reference: SK324634.

Required maps: Outdoor Leisure 24 (White Peak) or Pathfinder 761 (Chesterfield) both 1:25,000 scale. Alternatively, Landranger 119 Buxton, Matlock & Dovedale 1:50,000 scale

Terrain: Farmland, woodland, extensive views of the Amber valley and an ancient packhorse road, with some lengthy uphill (and downhill) stretches.

Refreshments: None (unless a diversion to the Kelstedge Inn is made - approx. 1 mile extra in total)

Approximate time: 2 hours and 45 minutes.

Public transport: None directly, but buses from Matlock and Chesterfield pass within half a mile of the starting point.

The Walk

The starting point at Eddlestow Lot picnic site ❶ is reached from the A632 Chesterfield - Matlock road by taking the road at the top of Slack Hill signposted for Beeley. Then after 500 yds, take the right turning (signposted) to the picnic site. The first half mile or so of the walk is on metalled roads, but these are quiet and have pleasant views.

Lake between Wilkin House and Peasunhurst

From the picnic site, turn right onto the lane and follow it downhill for almost half a mile until reaching a road junction near Jaggers' Cottage. Take the left turning, which is signposted "Beeley" and "Darley Dale". Follow uphill for nearly quarter of a mile, then take the signposted footpath on the right along a cart track. Stay on the cart track across several fields until reaching Shooters-Lea Farm ❸ (which has a pottery) where you will emerge onto the end of a lane near the farm entrance. Almost immediately cross the stile in the wall on the left. Keep to the right of the marshy field before reaching a wooden stile. The path turns right and almost immediately left (signposted), and passes in front of a cottage before emerging onto a farm track .

Stay on the farm track for about quarter of a mile, but leave it where it turns sharp right by continuing straight ahead around the left hand side of the field. After 150 yds look out for the stone stile on the left and cross next field diagonally towards the road (Hodge Lane). Take the path on the opposite side of the road and follow it through two fields keeping to the right. Cross the green next to Wilkin House Farm ❹, passing a pond to reach a stone stile. Go diagonally right behind the farm buildings to a near a gate. Head downhill, passing between two lakes and then uphill hrough the gate ahead, keeping to the right hand side of the large field as you climb gradually, reaching a stile in front of the cottages at 'easunhurst ❺.

Turn right onto the lane and follow it for about 50 yds, before turning right onto the blue waymarked footpath. Keep to the left of the field and at the end turn left at the stile, crossing the next field to the waymark post. Keep o the left of the following field before coming to a waymarked stile ahead. The next field is small, with a tendency to be overgrown, but continue ahead to a stone stile, and aim for the nearest group of trees, where there is a stile near an angle in the drystone wall.

lead uphill, keeping to the right of the stone marker post. As you reach he crest of the hill, you will be between two bands of trees. Aim for the extreme right of the left hand band and reach a stile, where you will be greeted with a picturesque view of the Amber valley. Proceed downhill owards Cullumbell Lane. Turn right and pass the post box and the former school, now Uppertown Social Centre, taking the stile into a field on the eft ❻.

'ollow the right hand side of the field to a stile and then across the centre of the next field to a gate, which leads into a short section of green lane. Continue into a small field and cross the stile in the right hand corner next o a gate. Ignore the path that goes diagonally right and stay to the left of he field. Cross over the stile formed by wooden slats nailed to two trees nto a large field. Keep to the left of the field until reaching an electricity post ❼.

Turn left down an embankment into woodland, following the path left hen right down to Smalley Brook. The path goes along the right hand bank for about 30-40 yds then crosses via stepping stones to the left hand side. It is easy to miss this crossing, so look carefully. Once over the stream, he path meanders through fairly dense vegetation before emerging into a meadow. On the far side of the meadow, the path follows the top of a bank, with a pond to the left and a cottage below on the right. Just after the cottage, drop down to a kissing gate, cross diagonally to another gate and urn right onto a lane ❽.

'ollow the lane downhill and then uphill to a T-junction where you turn eft. Ignore the first two paths on the right, before taking the red waymarked path after about 200 yds, by crossing a stile next to a gate.

Follow the path above scrubby woodland and, after about 300 yds, reach an iron gate leading onto the tree shaded Vernon Lane ❾.

If you wish to extend the walk and partake of refreshment at the Kelstedge Inn, turn left and follow this old packhorse road for about half a mile to Kelstedge, passing a lake (Bump Mill Dam) on the way. The Kelstedge Inn is situated on the main road (A632). Return by the same route.

Otherwise, turn right and follow the lane uphill, as it twists and turns, passing through old stone gateposts and fording a stream. Eventually, after a lengthy climb, the path emerges onto a chipping surfaced track. Bear right onto the track and at the end ❿ turn left onto the road climbing uphill back to the car park.

Vernon Lane

Places of Interest

Eddlestow Lot - The name either means 'Ædel's place' or 'splendid place', the latter being a good description of the view.

Jagger's Cottage - The name of this cottage is derived from the name given to the packhorse drivers, whose packhorse trains carried lead ore. There was a significant traffic in lead ore, and the metalled lane in front of the cottage forms part of the packhorse route from Ashover. Other types of packhorse driver were given names, including: 'Salters' who carried salt;

'Scotchmen' who carried Scottish linen and 'Badgers' who were itinerant traders (hence the phrase "stop badgering me").

Shooter's-Lea Farm - This farm is now a pottery, and dates from the 16th and 18th centuries.

Peasunhurst - This was a meeting place for Quakers in the 17th and 18th centuries. There is reputedly a Quaker burial ground behind the farmhouse. Quakerism had a strong following in the area around Uppertown from the late 17th century onwards. The name 'Peasunhurst' is derived from 'Pæga + stan + hyrst', which literally means "Pæga's stone in a copse". The name could refer to the small wood on the hillside, now called Roach Wood.

Cullumbell Lane - This lane is thought to be named after John Cullumbell, whose family was prominent in this area from the early 15th century onwards.

Uppertown Social Centre - This was previously the village school and was also used for religious services. The school closed in the late 1940s, but the building has been used as a social centre ever since.

Vernon Lane - This is part of the pack horse route from Ashover. There are still some sections with 'causeys' (paved with small flagstones) and old stone gate posts and markers.

Bump Mill Dam - If you take the optional extra route to Kelstedge, you will pass a lake, now stocked with fish and wild fowl, which was previously a mill dam. Bump Mill was a small cotton mill, which was situated close to Amber House. The mill is long since gone. The cotton would have been transported to Matlock by pack horse, as the Ashover Light Railway was not opened until 1925.

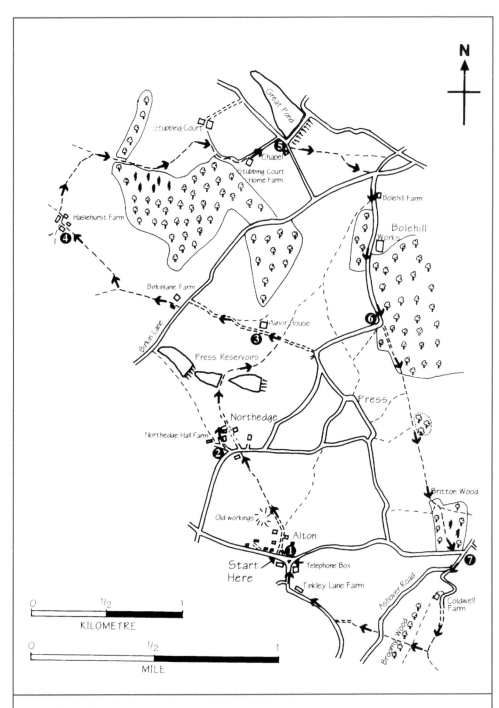

Walk 20 Alton - Press Reservoirs - Stubbing Court - Bole Hill - Britton Wood - Alton.

Route: Alton - Press Reservoirs - Stubbing Court - Bole Hill - Britton Wood - Alton.

Approximate distance: 7.5 miles (12 km)

Starting point: Alton, near Ashover.

Map reference: SK362643.

Required maps: Pathfinder 761 (Chesterfield) - 1:25,000 scale. Alternatively, Landranger 119 (Buxton, Matlock and Dovedale) - 1:50,000 scale.

Terrain: Farmland, woodland, Stubbing Court, The Great Pond of Stubbing and good views. Moderately strenuous, with some lengthy uphill stretches.

Refreshments: None.

Approximate time: 3 hours 45 minutes.

Public transport: None.

The Walk

This walk starts in the hamlet of Alton, which is about a mile and a quarter north east of Ashover. There is limited space for parking on the lane at its widest point near the Riding School and the post box, a short distance from the start of the walk ❶.

The walk starts opposite Honeycroft Farm, which has a sign on a wall advertising its pedigree herd of cattle. Take the stone track almost opposite the farm and go straight ahead past several cottages and houses. Continue along the track, forking left 75 yds after the last house. After another 100 yds, ignore the track that curves left and continue straight ahead between two dry stone walls (NB may be overgrown in summer). After a further 100 yds, enter a field and continue straight ahead, keeping close to the right hand side of the field until reaching a metal gate. Head towards the

Woodland at Bolehill

wide gap, then ahead to the squeeze stile. Cross half left a short distance to another squeeze stile, then turn right and follow the wall down to the farm and the road ❷.

Turn left along the road for 75 yds, then right onto a farm lane. After 50 yds bear right and keep just to the left of the barn conversion, crossing the stile behind it and then passing behind a timber livestock building and a stone barn. Reach a track and turn left onto it, heading downhill across fields towards the Press Reservoirs. Cross the dam wall of the middle reservoir and immediately bear half right and follow the top boundary of the field. Follow the path into the far corner of the field and go through an overgrown and bushy area, until reaching a stone stile. Emerge into a field and cross diagonally to a gap in the right hand corner which leads onto an unmade lane. Turn left and pass Manor House, which used to be the most remote pub in the area (alas, no more!) ❸.

Continue along the lane until reaching a metalled road (Birkin Lane). Turn left for 100 yds, then right onto a farm drive. Pass through the main gate, then through the gap at the metal gate on the left. Proceed ahead across two fields, keeping to the right hand wall. Reach a gate at a bend in the wall, pass through the gap and cross the centre of the next two fields. Then bear half right to a point halfway along the field, climb over the stile and cross towards the stone stile and gap, which is 30 yds down from the top of the field. Proceed straight ahead, keeping to the left hand side of three fields until reaching the farmyard of Haslehurst Farm ❹. Pass to the right of the large stone barn with the green tiled roof, through a gate and bear right and downhill across the centre of a large field. Cross the stone stile and follow the left side of the next field to a stile at the bottom left hand corner near a holly bush. Halfway across the next field, bear right. Head for the gate and stile on the edge of the woodland and cross the stile.

Stay close to the woodland across the first field. In the second, swing left towards the yellow waymark sign on a wooden post. Then go through the gap into the next field and keep to the right, reaching a stile at the end near the large beech trees. Head half right towards the stone wall ahead, then bear right along the wall. This is the parkland boundary of Stubbing Court, a fine country house, which unfortunately is not open to the public. Follow the boundary wall as it curves first left, then right and left again. Go past Stubbing Court Home Farm, and follow the straight lane downhill, eventually reaching a road and the Great Pond of Stubbing. (If you wish, you can get a good view of the Great Pond from the dam wall.)

At the road turn right and, 50 yds later, turn left at a gate near the Salem Methodist Chapel ❺. Follow the path (in places laid with flagstones) along the left hand side of two fields towards the rounded hill ahead. Cross a footbridge and climb around the right hand side of the rounded hill, reaching a stile at the crest on the right hand wall. Cross the road and head up the road opposite.

Follow this road (Bole Hill Lane) uphill through woodland for just over two thirds of a mile. Once over the crest of the hill, the road

Salem Chapel

veers sharp right ❻. Continue at this point directly ahead into pleasant woodland on a broad track. After quarter of a mile emerge into a field from the right hand corner of the wood. There are now excellent views east, south and west, with the spire at Clay Cross prominent half left. Continue along the ridge across three fields to Britton Wood. Fork left just inside the wood. The path drops slightly and then curves to the right and widens out. Continue through the wood to the lane at the far side. Turn left onto the lane, then immediate right at the T-junction ❼.

Follow the road for 75 yds, then take the lane on the left, which dips down at first. The lane zigzags uphill and passes in front of Coldwell Farm. Continue ahead on the grassy lane through a field to the gate at the far side. Beyond the gate, continue ahead for another 75 yds, then turn right 90° and head uphill towards Broomy Wood on the hilltop (NB You may find that the farmer sometimes ploughs the field, so the path may not be obvious). Go across the stile and drop downhill through the wood into a field and head down towards the metal gate.

Cross over the road and take the stile opposite (it may be partly hidden in summer) and climb uphill on the indistinct path towards the trees at the top. About 20 yds to the right of the trees, cross the timber stile. Turn left onto a farm track and follow this uphill to the gate and a lane. Turn right and follow the lane back into Alton, passing farm buildings and cottages and ignoring the lane on the left. Eventually, turn left at the triangular junction (with the telephone box) and return to your starting point.

View towards Alton from Bolehill

Places of Interest

Alton - The name means 'old farm' (from the Old English words 'ald' and 'tun'). Recent reports in the local press have revealed that villagers are often plagued by lost motorists, looking for Alton Towers, who have confused this village with the village of the same name in Staffordshire! Alton must have been quite religious in the 19th century as it had both a C of E chapel (built 1884) and a non-conformist chapel, both of which are no longer in religious use.

Manor House - Until quite recently, this was a public house, which was possibly the most hidden away and remote pub in the area. To reach this pub by car was not easy. All the roads in the vicinity are extremely narrow, the lane has gates and is unmade. Unless you knew about this place, you were very unlikely to stumble across it by accident. The inaccessibility, plus the limited opening hours probably account for why this is now a private residence. The building is an old manor house and dates from 1669. The initials over the doorway 'SS' refer to Samuel Sleigh, the original owner.

Stubbing Court - See Walk 15 for details.

The Great Pond of Stubbing - This was built in the 18th century by the Hunlokes of Wingerworth Hall.

Salem Independent Chapel - The name means 'Peace'. The chapel was built in 1849 and was founded by Joseph Fletcher, who worked at Wingerworth Ironworks. He was an evangelist who had previously preached at the Wingerworth School. With a rapidly increasing congregation, he had incurred the displeasure of the local clergy and Sir Henry Hunloke, who prevented him from preaching at the school. Fletcher easily raised the money to buy the land on which the chapel stands, but had to go outside the local area and to considerable expense to get the stone to build the chapel (Sir Henry owned all of the local quarries!). These days, the building is a Methodist Chapel.

Bolehill - The name, in common with several other hilltops in Derbyshire, is due to the lead smelting activity that took place in the past. From the 18th century, ironstone was quarried and transported down to Wingerworth. Also, building stone has been quarried on a small scale for many years. Today, the area is quiet and heavily wooded.

Bibliography

I have tried to compile as accurate a list of sources as possible, but inevitably I will have omitted some details of source materials, for which I apologise in advance.

Author	Title
Anon	The Link 1937 No 76 (Millthorpe Mill)
Auction Particulars	Rutland Estate - Particulars of Sale 1920
Battye, Kathleen M	Unstone - The History of a Village
Bright, Amos	Ford and the Ford Valley
Bright, Amos	A Trilogy of Murder
Bunker, Bessie	All Their Yesterdays
Cameron, K	The Place Names of Derbyshire
Christian, Roy	"Barlow" - DL&C Vol 58 1993
Christian, Roy	"Cartledge Hall" - DL&C Vol 31 - Jan/Feb 1966
Cutler, Nigel	"On the Packhorse Trail" - DL&C Vol 58 1993
Department of the Environment	List of Buildings of Historic Interest
Derbyshire Times	Various editions 1870 - 1995
Entwistle, Ronald	Holymoorside - Past and Present
Hopkinson, GG	Lead Mining in 18th Century Ashover
Kerry, Rev Charles	Reliquary New Series Vol 1 (Discovery of Skeletons at Overton Hall)
Lugard, C	The Inns and Outs of Ashover
Old Brampton WI	The Old Brampton Walk
Plant, KP	The Ashover Light Railway
Redfearn, Roger	"Linacre Enhanced" - DL&C Vol 33 1968
Redfearn, Roger	Chesterfield's Rural Fringe
Redfearn, Roger	"The Head of the Vale" - DL&C Vol 28 1963
Redfearn, Roger	"Whatever Happened to Barlow Hall?" - DL&C Vol 59 1994
Sheffield City Museums	Derbyshire Origins - A Field Guide to Archaelogical Sites in North Derbyshire
Sitwell, Sir George	Tales of My Native Village
Stubbs, Judith	A History of Cutthorpe
Tilley, J	Old Halls, Manors and Families of Derbyshire
Wingerworth Bulletin	December 82/January 83, April 83 and July 83

MH. November 1997.

THE FAMILY WALKS SERIES

Family Walks on Anglesey. Laurence Main	ISBN 0 907758 66 5
Family Walks around Bakewell & Castleton. Norman Taylor	ISBN 0 907758 70 3
Family Walks in Berkshire & North Hampshire. Kathy Sharp	ISBN 0 907758 37 1
Family Walks around Bristol, Bath & the Mendips. Nigel Vile	ISBN 0 907758 19 3
Family Walks around Cardiff & the Valleys. Gordon Hindess	ISBN 0 907758 54 1
Family Walks in the Cotswolds. Gordon Ottewell	ISBN 0 907758 15 0
Family Walks in the Dark Peak. Norman Taylor	ISBN 0 907758 16 9
Family Walks in Dorset. Nigel Vile	ISBN 0 907758 86 X
Family Walks in East Sussex. Sally & Clive Cutter	ISBN 0 907758 71 1
Family Walks on Exmoor & the Quantocks. John Caswell	ISBN 0 907758 46 0
Family Walks in Gower. Amanda Green	ISBN 0 907758 63 0
Family Walks in Gwent. Gordon Hindess	ISBN 0 907758 87 8
Family Walks in Hereford & Worcester. Gordon Ottewell	ISBN 0 907758 20 7
Family Walks on the Isle of Wight. Laurence Main	ISBN 0 907758 56 8
Family Walks around Keswick & Northern Lakeland. Timothy & Sylvia Bunker	ISBN 0 907758 93 2
Family Walks in the Lake District. Barry McKay	ISBN 0 907758 40 1
Family Walks in Leicestershire. Meg Williams	ISBN 0 907758 82 7
Family Walks in Lincolnshire. Camilla Harrison	ISBN 0 907758 67 3
Family Walks in Mendip, Avalon & Sedgemoor. Nigel Vile	ISBN 0 907758 41 X
Family Walks in Mid Wales. Laurence Main	ISBN 0 907758 27 4
Family Walks in the New Forest. Nigel Vile	ISBN 0 907758 60 6
Family Walks on the Norfolk Broads. Norman Taylor	ISBN 0 907758 90 8
Family Walks in Northamptonshire. Gordon Ottewell	ISBN 0 907758 81 9
Family Walks in the North Wales Borderlands. Gordon Emery	ISBN 0 907758 50 9
Family Walks on the North Wales Coast. Gordon Emery	ISBN 0 907758 89 4
Family Walks in North West Kent. Clive Cutter	ISBN 0 907758 36 3
Family Walks in the North Yorkshire Dales. Howard Beck	ISBN 0 907758 52 5
Family Walks in Oxfordshire. Laurence Main	ISBN 0 907758 38 X
Family Walks in Pembrokeshire. Laurence Main	ISBN 0 907758 75 4
Family Walks in Snowdonia. Laurence Main	ISBN 0 907758 32 0
Family Walks in South Derbyshire. Gordon Ottewell	ISBN 0 907758 61 4
Family Walks in South Shropshire & the Welsh Borders. Marian Newton	ISBN 0 907758 30 4
Family Walks in South Yorkshire. Norman Taylor	ISBN 0 907758 25 8
Family Walks in the Staffordshire Peaks & Potteries. Les Lumsdon	ISBN 0 907758 34 7
Family Walks around Stratford & Banbury. Gordon Ottewell	ISBN 0 907758 49 5
Family Walks in Suffolk. C. J. Francis	ISBN 0 907758 64 9
Family Walks in Surrey. Norman Bonney	ISBN 0 907758 74 6
Family Walks around Swansea. Raymond Humphreys	ISBN 0 907758 62 2
Family Walks in the Teme Valley. Camilla Harrison	ISBN 0 907758 45 2
Family Walks in Three Peaks & Malham. Howard Beck	ISBN 0 907758 42 8
Family Walks in the Weald of Kent & Sussex. Clive Cutter	ISBN 0 907758 51 7
Family Walks in West London. Caroline Bacon	ISBN 0 907758 72 X
Family Walks in West Sussex, South Downs & Coast. Nick Channer	ISBN 0 907758 73 8
Family Walks in West Yorkshire. Howard Beck	ISBN 0 907758 43 6
Family Walks in the White Peak. Norman Taylor	ISBN 0 907758 09 6
More Family Walks in the White Peak. Norman Taylor	ISBN 0 907758 80 0
Family Walks in Wiltshire. Nigel Vile	ISBN 0 907758 21 5
Family Walks in the Wye Valley. Heather & Jon Hurley	ISBN 0 907758 26 6
Family Walks in Birmingham & the West Midlands.	ISBN 0 907758 83 5

The publishers welcome suggestions for future titles and will be pleased to consider manuscripts relating to Derbyshire from new and established authors.

Scarthin Books of Cromford, in the Peak District, are also leading new, secondhand and antiquarian booksellers, and are eager to purchase specialised material, both ancient and modern.

Contact Dr. D.J. Mitchell 01629-823272

Visit our web site: **www.scarthinbooks.demon.co.uk**